MW01051650

STATE V. HODGMAN

Case File

Trial Materials

MW01051650

STATE V. HODGMAN

Case File

Trial Materials

Raam Wong
Senior Deputy Prosecuting Attorney
Seattle, Washington

NITA®
NATIONAL INSTITUTE FOR TRIAL ADVOCACY

© 2022 by the National Institute for Trial Advocacy

All rights reserved. No part of this work may be reproduced or transmitted in any form or by any means, electronic or mechanical, including photocopying and recording, or by any information storage or retrieval system without the prior written approval of the National Institute for Trial Advocacy unless such copying is expressly permitted by federal copyright law.

Law students who purchase this NITA publication as part of their class materials and attendees of NITA-sponsored CLE programs are granted a limited license to reproduce, enlarge, and electronically or physically display, in their classrooms or other educational settings, any exhibits or text contained in the printed publication or online at the proprietary website. However, sharing one legally purchased copy of the publication among several members of a class team is prohibited under this license. Each individual is required to purchase his or her own copy of this publication. See 17 U.S.C. § 106.

Address inquiries to:
Reprint Permission
National Institute for Trial Advocacy
325 West South Boulder Road, Suite 1
Louisville, CO 80027
Phone: (800) 225-6482
Email: permissions@nita.org

ISBN 978-1-60156-962-2
FBA 1962
eISBN 978-1-60156-963-9
FBA 1963

Printed in the United States of America

Official co-publisher of NITA.
aspenpublishing.com/NITA

CONTENTS

STATEMENT OF THE CASE

1) Synopsis

During violent demonstrations on the night of Daniel Stack's presidential inauguration, Mack Hodgman fired pepper spray into a crowd of far-left protesters. Jeremy Dane, an anarchist, responded by grabbing Hodgman and grappling over the pepper spray. Emily Hodgman, Mack's wife, intervened and shot Jeremy in the stomach. Emily claims she saw a knife in Jeremy's hand and needed to defend her husband. She is charged with assault in the first degree.

2) Statement of the Case

Friday, January 20, YR-3, was destined to be a volatile day in the history of Nita City, a liberal city in the Pacific Northwest. After prevailing in his extremely right-wing "Take Back America" presidential campaign, Daniel Stack was sworn in that morning. On that same evening, an alt-right provocateur named Maxi Rossi was speaking at the University of Nita. Rossi's college tour had been marred by large, violent demonstrations. Now, officials feared his appearance on the night of the inauguration was a tinderbox poised to ignite.

That evening, the line of ticketholders to see Rossi speak inside Blaine Hall stretched across Red Plaza. Many in the crowd wore Stack's signature "Take Back America" hats as they buzzed with jubilation over the political upheaval roiling the nation. But their celebratory mood was soon dampened. At about 6:20 pm, a procession of masked, black-clad Anti-Authoritarian Coalition ("Antiac") protesters marched into the square. The loose coalition of anarchists and other radicals formed a blockade that prevented access to the venue. As the evening wore on, the ticketholders mixed with the Antiac protesters, forming a dense mass of people pulsating with anger and frustration.

Into this chaotic stew walked Mack and Emily Hodgman. High school sweethearts, the couple bonded over video games, guns, and far-right YouTube videos. Emily went to the event with a handgun holstered beneath her coat. Mack immediately waded through the masses, gleefully challenging protesters. Mack soon got into a wrestling match with a protestor and then went around boasting that he had won the fight.

The final descent into disarray came when Antiac protesters jumped a young Maxi supporter named Ari Sinclair. The protesters pummeled Ari with a paint-filled ornament. Mack ran up to intervene. Emily followed close behind, reaching for her gun. Mack told Emily, "Calm down! Don't shoot anyone!" The police, meanwhile, did little to keep the factions apart as violence spread.

Then came bloodshed. The crime charged here was the result of a fast-moving chain of events. At about 8:24 pm, a middle-aged journalist with the Southern Poverty Legal Foundation named Dominic Nelson was filming the protest on their phone. An Antiac activist swatted the phone from Dominic's hands. Witnessing the altercation, Mack shot pepper spray toward the protesters who assaulted Dominic. Seeing this, a thirty-five-year-old anarchist named Jeremy Dane barreled through the crowd. Violently grabbing Mack's arm, Jeremy tussled over the pepper spray. Just then, a good Samaritan named Blake Fitzgerald intervened and pulled Jeremy off Mack. Seconds later, Emily stepped forward and shot Jeremy in the stomach. During the ensuing panic, Emily and Mack fled from the square. Jeremy was rushed to the hospital and survived.

Several hours later, the Hodgmans walked into police headquarters, proclaiming, "We're here to report a self-defense shooting." After briefly holding Mack Hodgman, the police released the couple. During a subsequent "queen-for-a-day" interview with the police, Emily claimed that she saw a knife in Jeremy's hand and feared he was about to "gut" her husband. After an investigation, the district attorney charged Emily Hodgman with assault in the first degree. Emily remains free on bail. Now, Jeremy refuses to testify. And the prosecution proceeds to trial without its star witness.

INSTRUCTIONS

Each party is limited to calling the following witnesses:

State of Nita:	Police Lt. Samuel Garcia, lead investigator
	Dominic Nelson, journalist and eyewitness
	Blake Fitzgerald, eyewitness
	Pat Sadie, expert in gaming and alt-right culture
Defendant:	Emily Hodgman, defendant
	Mack Hodgman, eyewitness and defendant's husband
	Ari Sinclair, teenaged eyewitness
	Brighton Stevens, forensic psychologist and ballistic expert

All years are stated in the following form:

YR-0 indicates the actual year in which the case is being tried (i.e., the present year);

YR-1 indicates the preceding year (use the actual year);

YR-2 indicates the second preceding year (use the actual year), etc.

The following stipulations are agreed upon by the parties:

1) The Facebook records were collected pursuant to a valid warrant.

2) The Facebook records are authentic.

3) Emily Hodgman is female. Jeremy Dane and Mack Hodgman are male. Other witnesses may be any gender.

4) The Twitter messages were sent from Jeremy Dane's account.

5) All lay witnesses can testify that the photos are fair and accurate representations of the events of January 20, YR-3.

6) Jeremy Dane refuses to honor a subpoena and will not testify.

Pretrial Orders:

1) The court denied Emily's motion to suppress the Facebook messages. The court held that statements made by Brendan and Mack are admissible to provide context for Emily's statements, which are admissible as an admission by a party opponent. See ER 801(d)(2).

2) Emily's motion to suppress Jeremy's statements moments after he was shot pursuant to the Confrontation Clause of the Sixth Amendment and *Crawford v. Washington*, 541 U.S. 36 (2004), was denied because the statements were nontestimonial and made in the course of an ongoing emergency. The statements are still subject to objection under the Rules of Evidence.

3) Each party's motion to exclude expert testimony was denied. The Court held that Pat Sadie and Brighton Stevens are both qualified as experts and their knowledge would assist the trier of fact to understand the evidence. Their testimony is admissible under either a *Frye* or a *Daubert* standard.

Electronic exhibits can be found at the following website:

http://bit.ly/1P20Jea
Password: Hodgman1

IN THE DISTRICT COURT OF THE STATE OF NITA
OF THE COUNTY OF DARROW

THE PEOPLE	)	
	)	
Plaintiff,	)	Case No. YR-3–62–80
	)	
v.	)	INFORMATION
	)	
EMILY ROSE HODGMAN,	)	
	)	
Defendant.	)	

The PEOPLE do accuse EMILY ROSE HODGMAN with the crime of Assault in the First Degree under the Code of Nita:

That the defendant EMILY ROSE HODGMAN in Darrow County on or about January 20, YR-3, with intent to inflict great bodily harm, did assault Jeremy Dane with a firearm, to-wit: shooting Jeremy Dane, a human being, in the abdomen, contrary to Chapter 9 of the Code of Nita.

DATED: February 19, YR-3

Kris B. Ford
Darrow County District Attorney

By: Emery Schiff
Senior Deputy District Attorney

County of Darrow

UNIVERSITY OF NITA

POLICE DEPARTMENT

20772 University Circle
Nita City, Nita 57829
819.555.6527
www.UNPD.nita

CASE INVESTIGATION REPORT—FINAL

TYPE OF CRIME: ASSAULT WITH FIREARM	VICTIM(s): JEREMY DANE
CRIME DATE/TIME: JANUARY 20, YR-3	SUSPECT(s): EMILY ROSE HODGMAN
AUTHOR: LT. SAM GARCIA #4345	CASE #: YR-3–00278

20 January YR-3

On this date, right-wing personality Maximus Rossi was scheduled to appear at the University of Nita during his "Dangerous Renegade" tour of college campuses. Mr. Rossi's earlier tour appearances had sparked large, sometimes violent, counterprotests. I was particularly concerned about the potential for unrest because the event was scheduled for the same day as the presidential inauguration of Daniel Stack. Anti-Stack protests were anticipated throughout the city. And online radical activists were using the hashtag #TurnBackStack and #DisruptJ20 on social media to promote violent disruption of January 20 events. I saw that one activist named JEREMY DANE tweeted several violent messages, including a retweet of a photo reading, "Stab Maxi, All Out J20!" (**Ex. A.1–2**). (Rossi was closely aligned with Stack during his "Take Back America" presidential campaign.) I do not know DANE's political affiliation.

Rossi was appearing in Blaine Hall's large auditorium located on Red Plaza, a sprawling square in the heart of campus that carries a long history of peaceful protest and free expression. At my direction, police erected fencing at the top of a short series of steps in front of Blaine to keep counterprotesters back. Twenty officers, including myself, assembled behind this fencing to check bags and control the flow of ticketholders into the building. Although I considered doing bag checks in the indoor foyer of the auditorium, I instead chose to have ticketholders line up in Red Plaza so we could check for weapons before they entered the building.

The tickets did not designate seats, so attendees began lining up well in advance of 1700, when the doors would open. Unfortunately, by 1800, the use of a single checkpoint had created a bottleneck, and hundreds of ticketholders were forced to stand in the frigid cold in a line that stretched across the square (**Ex. D**). At 1820, approximately 40 counterprotesters from the Anti-Authoritarian Coalition ("Antiac") marched with military precision into the plaza (**Ex. E**). They wore black facemasks, carried black-and-red Antiac flags and chanted "Turn Back Stack!" The Antiac activists menaced the ticketholders near the front of the line, then formed a human blockade at the top of the steps, blocking entrance to Blaine Hall (**Ex. R**). Ticketholders responded by yelling profanity and taunts at Antiac. Several of them attempted to storm the entrance but were shoved back down the steps by the Antiac activists. Outnumbered, we decided to prohibit further entry to the event. The line of ticketholders devolved into chaos as angry attendees began intermingling with and confronting the counterprotesters, leading to heightened tensions and the occasional verbal and physical altercation. We were unable to separate the factions because it would have been unsafe for officers to enter the crowd.

At 2026, a counterprotester ran up to the police line and frantically shouted, "A woman just shot an anarchist—pointblank! She had pigtails and glasses! She fired at the man because he was beating up her husband! We need help!" The counterprotester faded into the crowd and I never got a name. I pushed through the crowd and found a man dressed all in black, later identified as JEREMY DANE, lying in a pool of blood. I did not see a shooter. DANE was surrounded by a mob of protesters and civilian "street medics" who were dressed in black and wearing backpacks as they pulled at DANE's clothing in an effort to locate the wound. DANE had a gunshot wound to his abdomen. As I removed his leather jacket, a grip strengthener and a Benchmade folding knife (in the closed position) fell from one of the pockets. I placed the items back in the pocket. Apparently mistaking the grip strengthener for a weapon in the darkness, another officer broadcast over the radio: "Anarchist victim armed with brass knuckles and large knife." I could see DANE's hands were empty. There were no other weapons near him, though with the crowds and confusion, it was difficult to see. In a state of shock, DANE said he was trying to stop a fascist from pepper spraying his "comrades," and he wasn't trying to hurt anyone. Not knowing the extent of his injuries, paramedics removed DANE'S outer clothing, including his jeans, jacket, and boots, to search for gunshot wounds. They left the items on the ground before rushing him to the hospital.

I was made lead investigator. My sergeant informed me that the media was already asking if we had a suspect. Some witnesses whose names I neglected to record had told me they'd seen a short, pudgy Stack supporter in a black leather jacket, tan scarf, and yellow ball cap scuffle with the victim immediately before the shooting. (This description matches the man I later identified as MACK HODGMAN.) I provided the description to the media as a person of interest.

Meanwhile, the crowds prevented us from securing the scene, and several people trampled through DANE'S blood. I taped off the scene at 2130 and used the flashlight on my cell phone to search the ground for shell casings, bullets, or weapons but turned up nothing. (I was unable to use my police-issued flashlight because it fell from my belt and was lost in the dark during the bedlam that surrounded my efforts to assist DANE.) I did not bring in a K9 for a more thorough search because it was more important to identify the gunman. I also did not swab any of the blood since DANE was the only person hurt.

At 2140, I collected DANE's belongings from off the ground: a folding Leatherman utility tool in the closed position and contained in a leather case attached to the right side of the waistband of DANE's jeans (I later opened it to photograph its various tools) (**Ex. P**); the Benchmade folding knife that I saw fall out of the right pocket of DANE's jacket in the closed position (**Ex. O**); heavy, steel-toed boots stained with blue paint on the soles (**Ex. Q**); red-and-black bandana, knotted in the back, in the back pocket of jeans (**Ex. Q**); leather jacket with sharp studs covering shoulders and arms; black jeans; and a grip strengthener. I did not locate a cell phone.

I returned to headquarters, where I was met by reporters asking why police failed to keep the factions apart. At 2340, MACK and EMILY HODGMAN entered the station with their hands raised. MACK stated, "We're here to report a self-defense shooting." EMILY nodded. I handcuffed MACK. I did not observe any tattoos on his exposed forearms. MACK was limping and complaining of ankle pain. EMILY was polite and cooperative. EMILY handed me an American Girl Doll shopping bag and said, "Here are the weapons," but declined to provide a statement or explain what lead to the shooting. Hoping to put the public at ease, I announced to the media that a suspect was in custody. But after further consideration, I realized that the HODGMANS had not said who the shooter was or if it was even someone else who pulled the trigger. We released MACK and escorted him out the back door to avoid the media.

Inside the bag that EMILY handed me I located the following: Guardian Angel pepper spray gun (**Ex. N**); Glock semiautomatic pistol in a paddle holster (**Ex. M**); Karambit folding knife with a quick-draw ring (folded closed) (**Ex. L**). I did not inspect the pistol in the event it needed to be fingerprinted. I drafted a certification of probable cause for MACK.

I visited DANE at Oceanview Hospital. He was just out of surgery. DANE asked if he was under arrest and requested an attorney. A nurse stated DANE would require more surgeries, but the bullet would not be removed. DANE's friends, dressed all in black and carrying backpacks, were gathered in the hallway. They refused to provide their names, answer questions, or say if they had any of DANE's belongings.

21 January YR-3

This morning, I served a warrant on Facebook for any private messages sent by MACK from January 19–21, YR-3, and immediately received records showing a group chat between MACK, EMILY, and a BRENDAN KELLOG discussing plans for the Maxi event (**Ex. C.1–3**). I did not seek a warrant for EMILY's private messages since she was not yet a suspect. However, I did photograph her social media profile (**Ex. B**). After locating DANE's Twitter I also saved screenshots of DANE's tweets but did not seek a warrant for his private messages because there was no probable cause to believe he had committed an offense (**Ex. A.1–2**).

I also exchanged emails (Attachment A) with two potential eyewitnesses, DOMINIC NELSON and BLAKE FITZGERALD.

27 January YR-3

I interviewed DANE at the hospital with his attorney present. Although he was not in custody or considered a suspect, I Mirandized him in case I determined he was the aggressor. A true and correct copy of the interview transcript is included as Attachment B.

28 January YR-3

This evening, I watched an Action 10 News report featuring the police radio traffic in which one of the patrol officers described DANE as armed with a "large knife" and "brass knuckles." The radio traffic had been obtained through a public records request.

I interviewed NELSON and collected photos he took immediately after Antiac attacked a 17-year-old Stack supporter, later identified as ARI SINCLAIR (**Ex. G–H**). In one photo (**Ex. G, #2**), EMILY reaches beneath her jacket. The motion is consistent, in my training and experience, with reaching for a paddle holster.

1 March YR-3

I met with EMILY, her attorney, and Deputy DA Emery Schiff to conduct a "queen for the day" interview. EMILY signed the proffer agreement, included as Attachment C. EMILY admitted she was the shooter and claimed DANE was brandishing a knife. (EMILY did not mention a knife at the police station on January 20.)

After the interview, I called DANE, and he denied brandishing a knife. DANE confirmed that he was carrying the Leatherman tool and the Benchmade knife that we have in evidence. DANE also said he had a Griptilian knife clipped to his right pants pocket. He said the knife had a black handle and a serrated 3.45-inch blade coated black. He admitted that the length of the blade made it illegal to carry under Nita Municipal Code, but he denied drawing the knife. When I told DANE that the Griptilian was not recovered, he did not know how it was lost. DANE ended the conversation and said further contact should go through his attorney.

I received an email from a new witness, ARI SINCLAR. However, I did not collect a statement from him since he did not observe the shooting.

I redrafted the certification of probable cause naming EMILY as the shooter.

2 January YR-0

I spoke with DA SCHIFF and learned DANE was refusing to participate in a pretrial interview with EMILY HODGMAN's defense attorney. SCHIFF stated that the Court then ordered a deposition, but DANE did not appear. I drove by DANE's home to check on him. He was cordial but stated he would not appear unless the prosecution obtained a material witness warrant for him. SCHIFF indicated the prosecution would proceed to trial without DANE.

ATTACHMENT A—CASE #: YR-3–00278 REPORT

Samuel Garcia

From: Dominic Nelson <Dom.Nelson@splf.nita>
Sent: January 21, YR-3 11:20 PM
To: Lt. Samuel Garcia <s.garcia@unpd.nita>
Subject: RE: January 20 Incident

Lt. Garcia—I'm not sure how much I have to offer. I barely saw or heard anything because I was blinded by pepper spray at the time of the shooting. I have several more media interviews I need to complete, plus a meeting with my book agent. I should be done with those obligations by January 28 and can come to the station then. I'd love to see you nail this guy.

Warm regards,

Dominic Nelson
www.RadicalAlert.nita

From: Lt. Samuel Garcia <s.garcia@unpd.nita>
Sent: January 21, YR-3 11:10 PM
To: Dominic Nelson <Dom.Nelson@splf.nita>
Subject: January 20 Incident

Mr. Nelson,

I saw your interview on Action 10 News tonight regarding the events of January 20. Could you please let me know when you can visit the station for a recorded interview as I seek to bring charges against Mack Hodgman?

Lt. Samuel Garcia
University of Nita Police Department

Samuel Garcia

From:	Blake Fitzgerald <PumpItUp@fmail.nita>
Sent:	January 21, YR-3 8:30 PM
To:	Lt. Samuel Garcia <s.garcia@unpd.nita>
Subject:	RE: January 20 Event

Good evening, Lieutenant. I remember everything well. This Antiac guy in a black leather jacket was assaulting a right-wing extremist who had been shooting pepper spray. I managed to grab the Antiac guy and pull him back, but the spikes on his jacket made him difficult to hold and he broke my grip.

I'd be happy to come meet with you, but I'm studying for my nursing licensure exam at the moment. Would early March work?

Thanks!

Blake

From:	Lt. Samuel Garcia <s.garcia@unpd.nita>
Sent:	January 21, YR-3 8:00 PM
To:	Blake Fitzgerald <PumpItUp@fmail.nita>
Subject:	January 20 Event

Mr. Fitzgerald,

Thank you for leaving a message on the police department hotline about the events of January 20. Could you please let me know a good time to come by my office for an interview?

Lt. Samuel Garcia

University of Nita Police Department

Samuel Garcia

From:	Lt. Samuel Garcia <s.garcia@unpd.nita>
Sent:	March 1, YR-3 8:15 AM
To:	Ari Sinclair <captainari@cablecast.nita>
Subject:	re: Shooting in Red Plaza

Hello, Ari. I apologize for the delay in responding to your email. My investigation is focused on the person who committed the shooting. We cannot chase down every incident of lawlessness from that evening. Because you did not see the shooting itself, I do not need to interview you. We are about to close the case.

Lt. Samuel Garcia
University of Nita Police Department

From:	Ari Sinclair <captainari@cablecast.nita>
Sent:	January 22, YR-3 6:36 PM
To:	Lt. Samuel Garcia <s.garcia@unpd.nita>
Subject:	Shooting in Red Plaza

Dear Lieutenant Garcia:

I was in Red Plaza the other night and saw the leader of Antiac stirring up trouble. I believe he was conspiring with other activists to carry out violence against Stack supporters. I believe you may already know his identity if my suspicions are correct.

I don't know if the Antiac leader I saw had anything to do with the shooting. But what I do know is the protester who was injured probably had it coming and deserved to be shot.

I am still suffering memory loss as a result of an injury I suffered at the hands of Antiac, and I am fuzzy on many details. But I am happy to assist in your investigation.

Sincerely,

Ari Sinclair

UNIVERSITY OF NITA
POLICE DEPARTMENT

20772 University Circle
Nita City, Nita 57829
819.555.6527
www.UNPD.nita

WITNESS STATEMENT—DRAFT

TYPE OF CRIME: ASSAULT	VICTIM(S): JEREMY DANE
DATE/TIME OF INTERVIEW: JANUARY 27, YR-3	SUSPECT(S): EMILY HODGMAN
AUTHOR: LT. SAM GARCIA #4345	CASE #: YR-3–00278

LT GARCIA: Today's date is January 27, YR-3. I'm here at Oceanview Hospital for a recorded interview with Jeremy Dane. I'm here with Jeremy's attorney. Jeremy, do I have your permission to record?

DANE: Sure, have at it, Chief.

LT GARCIA: OK. Just to be safe, I'm gonna advise you of your rights. You have the right to remain silent. Anything you say can be used against you in court. You have the right to have a lawyer. If you cannot afford a lawyer, one will be appointed. Do you wish to speak to me?

DANE: I know my rights. I'll speak to you.

LT GARCIA: OK, can you start off by telling me a little about yourself?

DANE: I'm thirty-five years old, and I work as a computer security engineer here in town.

LT GARCIA: Let's talk about January 20. Start from the beginning.

DANE: Well, leading up to that night, I was mobilizing online resistance to Maxi's speech and the inauguration of Stack. But I only went to Red Plaza to observe the protests and help keep the peace. I myself wasn't there to protest. While I consider myself an anarchist, I am not a member of Antiac. I do belong to the Socialist Rifle Cooperative of Greater Nita City and the World-wide Workers General Defense Association. The WWGDA is an anti-fascist organization that covers legal bills for protesters. I probably shouldn't have told you that.

LT GARCIA: Were you armed?

DANE: No, I was not armed. I was carrying a few things I use for work. Let's see, I had my Benchmade folding knife in my right pocket and Leatherman utility tool in a case attached to my waist, maybe some other items. I always carry them. They're handy for cutting cable at work. What's it to you? I imagine I wasn't supposed to have them on campus, but I didn't take them out all night.

LT GARCIA: OK, so can you tell me what happened?

DANE: All night I was trying to de-escalate conflict. As the evening wore on, I kept seeing this tubby guy in a leather jacket and a yellow hat picking fights with protesters and shooting pepper spray into the crowd at random. Right before I was shot, he starts pepper spraying several of my Antiac allies and ends up hitting a journalist named Dom Nelson. Dom is someone I follow on Twitter. I ran up and yelled, "Give me the pepper spray. Or else I'm gonna get it from you." I kept grabbing the right side of his body, shaking and tussling him around pretty hard. I recognize that you could probably charge me with a crime for using that kind of force. But it's what I needed to do to get the guy to drop the pepper spray.

LT GARCIA: What happened next?

DANE: That's when I heard the gunshot and felt a piercing sensation in my stomach. I'm not sure how I got to the ground. I didn't see who shot me. I've got black spots in my memory.

LT GARCIA: How are you doing now?

DANE: I've got a long road ahead of me. The bullet entered my stomach, passed through my lungs, and lodged next to my spine. I lost my gall bladder and half my colon. I've lost track of how many surgeries I've had.

LT GARCIA: What would you like to see happen?

DANE: You know, my getting shot is a manifestation of violent political ideologies. And it's completely upended my life. I am not going to inflict more damage on someone else by participating in this process. Incarcerating someone is just as destructive as what happened to me. You should read "Slavery by Another Name." Watch the documentary "13th." You'll see what our criminal justice system is really about. If the people who shot me wish to engage in restorative justice, I would meet with them. I have sympathy for them. I'd like to see our community engage in a constructive dialogue. But I'm not going to escalate violence by assisting in prosecution by testifying. I refuse to be like them.

LT GARCIA: I understand, Jeremy. Anything else you want us to know?

DANE: That's about it.

LT GARCIA: OK, I'll turn off the recorder. It's still January 27, 1430 hours.

Darrow County District Attorney's Office

Service with Integrity

March 1, YR-3

Emily Rose Hodgman
740 Clancy Street NW, Apt. 305
Nita City, NI 98105

Dear Ms. Hodgman:

You have indicated a desire to provide information which would be of assistance in the criminal investigation and potential prosecution of a shooting that occurred January 20, YR-3, at the University of Nita. The terms of the contemplated proffer agreement are set forth below:

1) You will submit to a recorded interview, with the assistance of counsel, about your knowledge of the events. The interview will be conducted by Deputy District Attorney Emery Schiff and University of Nita Police Lt. Sam Garcia.

2) The State may not use your statements against you in a criminal trial in its case in chief. However, your statements may be considered and relied upon in forming an expert opinion by any expert that the State may choose to retain. Your statements can also be used against you for purposes of cross-examination, should you choose to testify.

3) The State may make derivative use of your statements to pursue further investigation. Any evidence derived from the proffer may be used against you in a trial or other proceeding.

4) While you wish to receive some benefit by cooperating with the State, you expressly understand that the government is making no promise of any consideration at this time.

This letter constitutes the full and complete agreement of the parties. Neither you nor the State will incur additional obligations as a result of this agreement.

Kris Ford 3/1/YR-3
Kris B. Ford
Darrow County District Attorney

Acknowledged and Agreed to: *Emily A. Hodgman 3/1/YR-3*
Emily Rose Hodgman

ATTACHMENT D—CASE #: YR-3–00278 REPORT

UNIVERSITY OF NITA

POLICE DEPARTMENT

20772 University Circle
Nita City, Nita 57829
819.555.6527
www.UNPD.nita

CASE INVESTIGATION REPORT—ADDENDUM

TYPE OF CRIME: ASSAULT WITH FIREARM	**VICTIM(S):** JEREMY DANE
CRIME DATE/TIME: JANUARY 20, YR-3	**SUSPECT(S):** EMILY ROSE HODGMAN
AUTHOR: LT. SAM GARCIA #4345	**CASE #:** YR-3–00278

TRAINING AND EXPERIENCE

I am providing this addendum at the request of Ms. Hodgman's attorneys to explain my training and experience.

I completed basic training at the Criminal Justice Academy in YR-7 and have received updated training in Interrogation, Scene Photography, Basic Scene Investigation, and Evidence Collection. I was promoted to my current role as the Investigations Unit lieutenant in December YR-4. My duties include screening social media for potential threats to the campus community.

WITNESS STATEMENTS

STATEMENT OF BLAKE FITZGERALD[1]

My name is Blake Fitzgerald. I'm twenty-five years old and work as a nurse. My passions are what I like to call "the three P's": pumping iron, physical fitness, and peace. On January 20, I was midway through the "power" phase of my weight training. The workouts build explosive power and stamina through a small number of reps at maximum weight. A good workout leaves me swollen and feeling exceptionally strong. Diet is everything! I consume 3,500 calories and eat five meals per day. My diet includes protein shakes—kale, beef liver, and egg yolks—and lean chicken, tuna, and hardboiled eggs. I'm 6'0'' and 240 pounds. My chest is 58 inches, biceps 22 inches, and thighs 30 inches.

I got into some trouble as a young man. I was convicted of three counts of felony theft for shoplifting creatine five years ago. It was a period of time when I was struggling to make ends meet. I'm still a good person and, while I did wrong, those acts don't define me. I was convicted before Judge Ernie Mixon in the Nita Municipal Court and sentenced to forty hours of community service. I was also convicted of misdemeanor false statement when I was sixteen for giving a fake name to a school resource officer. Ten years ago, I was detained but not charged for vandalism during the anti-World Trade Organization protests that I participated in.

I went to Red Plaza on January 20 to help keep the peace. While I've been to anarchist meetups in the past, I wasn't supporting either side that night. Heck, I was a "Barney Bro." But I've witnessed violence at these events before. Too many people stand around and do nothing. I'd seen on the news that violent Antiac protesters had harassed attendees at other Maxi events. So, I hoped to use my physical advantages and 24-inch biceps to help keep people safe. I'm a peacemaker—peace through strength. Maxi and every one of his supporters who were there that night are repulsive. They should be kicked to the curb. I mean that metaphorically—everyone deserves to be safe. As disgusting as they are, though, the Constitution gives them the right to assemble peacefully.

That evening, I completed a monster workout and then headed to Red Plaza. The atmosphere was already charged when I arrived. An Antiac mob, dressed like punk rockers, was blocking the entrance to Blaine Hall. They chanted, "No Stack! No Way! No Fascist USA!" They threw glass bottles and bricks at the Maxi ticketholders, who were like sitting ducks in that long line. They were wearing red hats and yelling back, "Stack! Stack!" and "Take Back America!"

Police eventually shut down the event because of all the chaos and fear Antiac was causing. The line to get in dissolved and the two sides began mixing. Arguments turned to pushing and then punching and pepper spray. The cops just cowered behind their barricades, watching as the Antiac activists grew more dangerous. I'm a big guy, but even I felt claustrophobic and scared

---

1. The transcript of the witness's interview with the police was excerpted so that only the witness's answers are reprinted here. Assume that this is a true and accurate rendering of Mr. Fitzgerald's answers. The recorded interview was conducted in person on March 1, YR-3 at police headquarters by Lt. Sam Garcia.

standing in the middle of the crowds that were packed near the entrance to Blaine Hall. Still, once you stepped away from the masses, it was obvious that most of the plaza was empty and it would've been easy to leave if you wanted to avoid trouble.

I recognized Mack and Emily Hodgman from the media coverage. On the 20th, I saw the two of them throughout the night. At first, Mack was wearing a red Take Back America hat; he switched to a yellow hat later. He stood out because he was literally elbowing his way through clusters of Antiac protesters. He was hyper-aggressive. I never saw him assault anyone, flash a weapon, or throw the first blow. But he kept shoulder-checking protesters, tapping them on the back, and getting in their personal space, all under the guise of merely moving through the crowd. People would tell Mack to back off, and he'd get in their face and belligerently say, "Stack's your president now too" or to call them "socialist." I assumed he was itching for a fight. Emily was his backup. As he worked his way through the crowds, she trailed very close behind him. She was hunched down a bit and had her hand on Mack's shoulder, kind of like you see military police do in a raid. She had an anxious grin on her face like all hell was about to break loose.

Jeremy Dane stuck out as well. He looked like your quintessential Antiac extremist with his black jeans, steel-toed combat boots, and nose piercing. He was wearing this black leather jacket with sharp metal studs all around the sleeves and shoulders. If you ask me, he looked like he was auditioning for a Judas Priest cover band. I never saw Jeremy wear a face mask or chant with Antiac, but he could easily be mistaken for Antiac in the way he was dressed and carrying himself. I saw him circling the groups of right-wingers with his chest puffed out like some sort of tough guy. Jeremy got involved in a couple little scuffles with Maxi supporters, but it was hard to tell if he was the instigator or was serving as one of the "peacekeepers" that were trying to break things up. There was so much chaos that it was impossible to tell anyone's intentions.

I'll never forget the moments leading up the shooting. At about 8:15 pm, a couple hundred people from both sides were tightly packed near the flagpole on the Diagram. There was a lot of jostling and yelling going on. Mack and several other right-wingers started taunting protesters with a Jorge the Toad flag **(Ex. G, #1)**, a highly offensive symbol, about ten feet away from me. They were smiling and singing, and mostly seemed to be having a good time. Jeremy was nearby. He walked in front of them and made the devil horns gesture with both hands **(Ex. G, #2)**. From the looks of it, his hands appeared to be empty in that moment, but I didn't get a good look.

Seconds later, I looked to my right and saw a pack of Antiac thugs giving an older journalist a hard time. They weren't assaulting him, per se. But they were harassing him and at one point, they knocked out of his hands a selfie stick with a cell phone camera attached. Antiac is hostile towards members of the press who might reveal their identifies. Just then, Mack ran up with Emily trailing close behind, her hand still on his shoulder like they were going into combat or something. Mack struck a silly pose, with one foot in front of the other, and squirted orange pepper spray at some Antiac activists harassing the journalist. Mack was wearing this gleeful smirk as he was shooting his little spray gun. Emily said, "Proud of my man!" I couldn't figure out why Mack was being so provocative. The journalist didn't appear to be in any danger. Mack was a terrible shot and the spray got on some innocent bystanders. Mack's pepper spray drove the crowd's energy into overdrive, and I feared a riot. I was gagging from the pepper spray and my eyes were burning. I could barely see. I managed to yell at Mack, "Put the damn pepper spray away!"

Just then, Jeremy bashed through the crowd like a raging bull and attacked Mack from behind, knocking Emily backwards. **Exhibit J, #1** captures the moment as Jeremy grabbed Mack by his hoodie with his left hand and tried to reach around Mack's body for the pepper spray with his right. My vision was still limited from the effects of the pepper spray, but I could hear Jeremy yell, "What the hell are you doing, fascist? I'm gonna git you!" Or maybe he said, "git It *from* you." It was difficult to hear over the loud chants of "Antiac! Antiac! Antiac!" all around us. Mack was playing keep-away with the pepper spray. Emily looked absolutely terrified.

Next, in **Exhibit J, #2**, you can see that Mack then broke free, turned to the left, and stepped away from Jeremy with a big smile on his face. With his back turned towards Jeremy, Mack was doing something with his hands. A couple of right-wingers managed to briefly block Jeremy from Mack. But Jeremy effortlessly pushed them aside and charged at Mack again, as seen in **Exhibit J, #3**. Emily is in the foreground in pigtails.

Jeremy spun Mack around to face him. Jeremy pulled on Mack's right forearm with his left hand in the direction of crowds of Antiac thugs who were now closing in and far outnumbering the right-wingers. Jeremy wasn't exactly throwing haymakers or kicking Mack, at least that I could see. And from my angle, Jeremy appeared unarmed. I have no idea what Emily saw from where she was standing. Mack wasn't doing anything to defend himself or crying out for help. But there was a clear disparity in athleticism and force between the two men. And I could tell Mack was in real jeopardy and could easily be pulled into the mob and beaten.

With no time to weigh my options, I acted on instinct. **Exhibit K, #1** captures the next moment as I grabbed Jeremy from behind, with a hand on each bicep, and pried him off Mack. The red circle shows my hand gripping Jeremy's bicep. The expression on my face is me straining to pull Jeremy back. To my right, there was a masked Antiac member charging in to finish Mack off. Mack was waving a brown scarf with his left hand. I still don't know what was in his right. You can just barely make out Emily extending her left arm towards Jeremy.

Exhibit K, #2 shows the next moment, maybe two seconds later, when I've completely pulled Jeremy off Mack. Jeremy was still struggling and driving at Mack. But I held him tight. Mack was no longer in danger. Emily would have no way of knowing this, but because I'd been beasting up at the gym, I had the power necessary to hold Jeremy tight. He never broke my grip. Jeremy may be a tall, strong guy, but he's no match for my 30-inch biceps. **Exhibit K, #2** appears to show something around Mack's ring finger, but I'm not sure what it was. I heard someone yell, "He's got a knife!" but I didn't know who that was referring to. In the photo, you can see Emily moving in with her left arm lifted high but angled down towards Jeremy's stomach.

Just then, I heard a loud bang and felt Jeremy's body tremble. The force instantly drained from his body. People were shouting, "They shot him!" and calling for a medic. As I placed Jeremy on the ground, I looked up in the direction of the bang, and saw Emily staring intently towards Jeremy's lifeless body. Emily had a calm, steely expression on her face. She was reaching her left hand behind the back of her jacket. I looked down at Jeremy in my arms. His face was ashen, his eyes glassy and vacant. I looked back up, and Emily and Mack were gone. The whole incident lasted maybe twenty seconds.

Street medics ran up with gauze and rubber gloves. They lifted Jeremy's shirt and exposed a bloody wound in the middle of his stomach. I could feel Jeremy's labored breaths and see beads of sweat form on his forehead. It felt like an eternity before the cops appeared, but it was only a minute or two. They grabbed our shirt collars and pulled us away from Jeremy and rendered first aid. I heard Jeremy mumble, "I was trying to help my friends, and a fascist shot me. I wasn't trying to hurt anyone." I couldn't make out in the darkness if anything was lying on the ground next to Jeremy. They removed Jeremy's clothes to look for gunshot wounds before loading him onto a Gator cart and carrying him out of the square.

The next day, I read in the *Nita Times* that Mack was the suspected shooter and he was claiming self-defense. That's insane. They could've killed someone—they could've killed me. It was completely unnecessary. Mack was no longer in jeopardy after I pulled Jeremy away. I then called the police department and exchanged the emails dated January 21, YR-3, with Lt. Garcia.

STATEMENT OF DOM NELSON[2]

My name is Dom Nelson and I'm sixty years old. I'm presently the writer and videographer for a blog called Radical Alert, which is published by the Southern Poverty Legal Foundation. I monitor and expose far-right activities in support of SPLF's mission to resist bigotry in America by exposing hate groups to the public, the media, and law enforcement.

We pride ourselves on working closely with law enforcement and reporting crime to the police within twenty-four hours. I have written three books about the alt-right. Sales are disappointing, and I struggle to get free media. I'm sorry I couldn't meet with you earlier, Lt. Garcia. After the shooting, I was swamped with TV interviews and meetings with my publisher. They've offered a $40,000 advance on a book I'm planning about this case. My publisher said it was important to raise my profile in support of the book. The SPLF promised to profile me on their homepage if the shooter is brought to justice through a successful trial. Once I realized how much press the shooting was getting, I knew the investigation was important and decided to come forward.

I went to Red Plaza to report on the link between Maxi Rossi, Daniel Stack, and the alt-right. Maxi is a provocateur who loves to wind liberals up with his brand of hateful, xenophobic speech. He likes to say the best response to "outrage culture" is to be outrageous. Maybe that explains his taste for fur coats, designer sunglasses, and bleached hair. Maxi is aligned with The Upright Men, a far-right extremist group whose members sometimes serve as his bodyguards.

I arrived in Red Plaza at about 5 pm on January 20, YR-3. I observed a couple hundred ticketholders wearing red Take Back America hats in a long line that snaked across Blaine Hall. After covering dozens of these events, I was shocked to see the police force the attendees to stand outside where they'd be like sitting ducks for counterprotesters. The police should have had the ticketholders wait inside the building, or at least keep them cordoned off from the protesters. Instead, the police risked the personal safety of the attendees who were there trying to exercise their right to free speech and assembly.

Several dozen masked Anti-Authoritarian Coalition members began marching into the square around 6:20 pm. They marched past a sign that read, "University Property. No Guns, Knives, or Weapons." "Antiac" is a coalition of anarchists and other leftist radicals who engage in intimidation and physical confrontation at far-right rallies. Many civil rights groups are critical of their violent tactics. But I reject attempts to claim equivalence between Antiac and the far-right. Antiac rejects bigotry but uses questionable tactics. The alt-right embraces evil ideology and uses extreme violence. I am very much opposed to the alt-right and anyone who subscribes to that ideology.

---

2. The transcript of the witness's interview with the police was excerpted so that only the witness's answers are reprinted here. Assume that this is a true and accurate rendering of Mr. Nelson's answers. The recorded interview was conducted in person on January 28, YR-3 at police headquarters by Lt. Sam Garcia.

When Antiac arrived, they crowded the event ticketholders from both sides while wielding red-and-black flags and anti-Maxi signs mounted on sticks that could easily have been used as weapons. They chanted, "Turn Back Stack!" as they formed a human blockade in front of Blaine Hall that effectively shut down the event. It was a sad day for free speech. I saw several Antiac members remove paint-filled water balloons and other projectiles out of black backpacks they were carrying and hurl them at the ticketholders. They were yelling things like, "America was never great" and "Shut it down!" Several Antiac activists waded among the ticketholders and instigated heated arguments. Some escalated into shoving matches; peacekeepers quickly broke those up. Eventually, many of the ticketholders went home and the ones who were left were outnumbered by the Antiac hooligans.

I know the gunshot victim, Jeremy, because I follow him on Twitter. I don't know if he's a member of Antiac—they're pretty secretive—but his posts certainly support their cause. It'd be absurd to call him their leader. Antiac is fundamentally anarchist and doesn't have a leadership structure. It would've been easy to mistake Jeremy for an Antiac member because he was wearing all black and had a circle-A anarchist tattoo on his neck. But I knew better because I watched him all night. At no point did I see Jeremy mask up like the other Antiac activists, and I didn't see him join in their intimidation tactics. In fact, Jeremy was serving as one of the so-called peacekeepers trying to deescalate conflict. He'd see two people about to come to blows and place his body between them until they calmed down. I spent most of the evening standing near Jeremy. I thought his tall, imposing figure and shaved head would keep trouble at bay.

Mack Hodgman caught my eye because he was a BIPOC (Black, Indigenous, and people of color) individual wearing a red Take Back America hat in a sea of Maxi's white supporters. That's not surprising. The alt-right's message of male resentment and outrage draws a wide spectrum of adherents. Mack was aggressively elbowing his way through the peaceful protesters, calling them "snowflakes," just daring them to fight. Mack was smirking and having the time of his life. I could see Emily following close behind him, clutching his shoulder and appearing anxious about Mack's antics.

At one point, Mack injected himself into one brief dustup involving a seventeen-year-old Maxi supporter who said his name was Ari. The kid got too close to a cluster of masked Antiac activists who snatched his hat and hit him in the face with a water balloon filled with blue paint. The police had a clear view of the kid get whacked from their elevated position on top of the steps, but they did nothing. The cops were absolutely useless and contributed to an atmosphere of anarchy and danger. Ari took several steps back after he was attacked but continued to posture in the direction of his attackers with his chest out. His dad stood at his side in a leather jacket. Things quickly calmed down. But then I saw Mack, no longer wearing a red hat, run up to the Antiac activists who had attacked Ari and stretch out his arms **(Ex. G, #1)**. Mack was ostensibly playing peacemaker by trying to defuse the situation. But if you want my opinion, he was trying to bait Antiac into a fight by getting right in their faces, just daring them to hit him. That's a common tactic among alt-right street fighters like the Upright Men. They provoke their opponents, particularly Antiac, into a fight and then claim self-defense. That said, I have no reason to believe Mack was an Upright Man.

As Mack antagonized Antiac, I photographed Emily frantically run up to him with her right hand beneath the back of her coat near her lower back **(Ex. G, #2)**. Mack turned around, saw where she was reaching, patted her shoulders, and reassured her: "Everyone's safe. Calm down! Don't shoot anyone!" That blew my mind. A kid gets tagged with a little paint, and she's about to fire into a crowd? I never saw Emily actually pull out her gun. And unlike Mack, she wasn't starting fights. But all I could think was if her threshold for danger is that low, she should not be carrying a gun! Who brings a gun to a demonstration?

Mack's behavior only escalated. I photographed Mack as he turned to a tall guy in a red Take Back America hat and yelled, "They have to start it!! When they start it, we go!" **(Ex. H)**. He looked like one of those guys who's a little too agro on the paintball field. Emily stood nearby and nodded in agreement. Mack then bear-hugged Ari, called him "Battle Brother" and let out a mighty roar that sounded like a battle cry. Emily half-heartedly played along, saying, "We won't stand for this!" They both seemed thirsty for revenge.

The shooting happened at about 8:20. By this point, the two sides had dissolved into one heaving mass of anger and noise, with a lot of pushing, yelling, and name-calling. I was standing at the flagpole filming the scene on my phone. Mack, now wearing a yellow hat, was standing near a cluster of red-hatted Maxi supporters who had unfurled a flag showing Jorge the Toad cartoon character **(Ex. I, #1)**. Jorge has been appropriated by the alt-right and become a symbol of intolerance. The image often provokes fierce reactions from opponents, which is probably the idea.

Anyway, just then, some masked Antiac idiots came up and swatted my phone off its selfie stick. This was the third time they had assaulted me like this that evening. Antiac tries to conceal its identity and takes issue with being photographed. My phone fell to the ground. I bent over to retrieve it as they continued to kick it around like a hockey puck, just inches from my head. I struggled to locate my phone in the darkness. Just then, I got a snootful of someone's pepper spray and began coughing and wheezing. My eyes swelled up and burned. I could barely see.

As I struggled to get my bearings, I could barely make out Jeremy and Mack fighting. Jeremy is tall and seemed to have the advantage over Mack, who was considerably shorter and pudgy. Jeremy looked pretty fierce and was yelling something about "getting" or "gutting" Mack. Because of the crowds, I could only see them from the chest up. Mack was still smiling and waving a tan scarf. I can say with complete certainty that there was no weapon in Jeremy's hands, though someone did yell, "He's got a knife!" But I couldn't tell who that was referring to.

Suddenly, I heard gunfire. Jeremy slumped over in the arms of a guy who looked like a body builder. I saw Emily after it was all over. She had her left hand beneath the back of her jacket as smoke wafted around her. She was staring at Jeremy's lifeless body with an unflinching and determined look. I did not see a gun. Police didn't arrive to aid Jeremy for several minutes.

I walked to my car. I knew I had important information to share but figured I could wait to call the authorities until things calmed down. I got lost trying to find my Prius. My vision was still affected from the pepper spray. I even tried to unlock the wrong car! As I was walking, I saw the Hodgmans at a bus stop. Mack told his wife, "Let's jump on this one!" and then hustled her onto a bus. I saw Mack had ditched his yellow hat on a bus bench.

I've visited Jeremy several times since this happened. He was in the hospital for about three weeks and underwent countless surgeries. I now consider him a friend. Cable news producers recently reached out to me to see if I could convince Jeremy to come on their show. I was hoping it'd be an opportunity to promote my books. But Jeremy declined. Jeremy also told me he intended on ignoring the subpoena to testify because of his objections to the criminal justice system. The January 21, YR-3, email fairly and accurately reflects what I wrote to Lt. Garcia.

EMILY HODGMAN PROFFER INTERVIEW[3]

My name is Emily and I'm twenty-two years old. I met my husband, Mack, in middle school. One day after school he called and said he liked me. I said I liked him back, and we've been two peas in a pod ever since. I had a difficult childhood. My parents fought over money and struggled to find work. At seventeen, my mom wanted me to be independent and asked me to move out. Fortunately, Mack's family took me in. He's my Disney prince.

After high school I went to work as a bank teller counting other people's money. Mack found a job installing floors, which he eventually lost after the economy turned south. I grew resentful that corrupt bank CEOs made gobs of money, and then get bailed out by the government, while we can't put food on the table. Our plan was for Mack to enroll in college and then become a doctor. I was going to stay home and raise the children we hoped to have. Our dream fell apart when Jeremy tried to kill my husband. I lost my job after my name was published in the paper and Antiac targeted my employer by hacking bank servers. Our whole life will be over for good if I'm convicted. How much more does the government want from us?

Our passion is tabletop fantasy games, like *Kings of the Dark Ages*. We assemble and paint all our own miniature warriors. My main character is Sandra the Slayer, a warrior-queen of the Helman clan who vanquished invading Vikings. We also play first-person shooter games on the internet with gamers from all over. Mack and I were loners in high school, didn't have a lot of friends. Video games have provided us with a whole community of friends and a platform to talk about gaming, debate current events, and just be ourselves with like-minded people.

I was never political until I was introduced to Maxi. I remember watching one of my favorite gamers, PizziePie, compete in a tournament on YouTube. When it was over, a Maxi video popped up in my recommended video feed. He was over-the-top, with frosted hair and wearing a hot-pink fur jacket. He was talking about how feminists were attacking our gaming culture because it's dominated by men. Well, I'm a woman and I play video games. I started following Maxi's "GamerGate" hashtag and was led to other alternative voices on YouTube and message boards. I "liked" some of that stuff on Facebook and joined some groups that sounded interesting.

We were introduced to The Upright Men through memes and videos posted online. Mack and I were impressed with how committed they were to the Western values and how they stood up to the protesters who sometimes appeared at Maxi events. Mack seemed smitten with The Upright Men. But like fantasy roleplaying games, Mack was merely pretending to be an Upright Man online. It was all make-believe and never went further than the internet. Mack was merely showing off for his fellow online "Battle Brothers" like Brendan Kellog. Brendan is a manly-man that Mack's always trying to impress. I've read on the internet that the Upright Men wear black

---

3. The transcript of Emily Hodgman's proffer interview with the police and the prosecution was excerpted so that only her answers are reprinted here. Assume that this is a true and accurate rendering of her statements. The recorded interview was conducted in person on March 1, YR-3, in her attorney's office.

and tan and follow a four-step initiation process, like taking an oath and memorizing a bunch of 80s movies. I learned yesterday that the fourth level involves fighting Antiac.

I joined the private Upright Girls Facebook group because of Mack. I agree that we need to stand up to those who attack our Western culture. But I only joined the group to share recipes and Crossfit tips and to commiserate with like-minded women. We only recently learned that the FBI had temporarily classified the Upright Men as domestic terrorists that were encouraging actual violence. Mack and I want no part of that. We unequivocally condemn violence and hatred by both sides.

The Facebook records are fair and accurate copies of my profile and conversation with Brendan and Mack. The timestamps appear to be accurate. I used an app on my phone to send those messages. The messages have been taken out of context by the media's biased coverage of the attack on my husband. When I wrote that I wanted to put anarchists "in their place," I meant I was ready to stand up for traditional values. I've seen *"deus vult"* on some memes posted on a Reddit message board. The expression—"God wills it"—resonated with me as a person of faith. When I said Mack was going for "level four," that had nothing to do with The Upright Men. I was referring to moving up a level in the game Viking Quest. Mack was being provocative in the messages, but I am offended by the idea that I am somehow responsible for my husband's actions.

I began carrying a gun every day after I witnessed a shootout between police and a carjacker. It was so terrifying. Since then, every morning I make Mack promise me he won't die that day. The world's a scary place—I imagine an attacker around every corner. So I took charge and got my concealed weapon permit. The only way to stop a bad guy with a gun is a good guy with a gun. Carrying is a responsibility. I've completed FBI shooting drills and read self-defense books. My favorite is *Fatal Engagement* by Mark Arans. It teaches you to aim for the midsection in a self-defense situation because that's the biggest, easiest target. When you're in danger, you rely on what Arans calls the five "S's" of escalation of force: shout for the attacker to stop, show your weapon, shove them back, shoot to warn, and then finally, shoot. If the threat is immediate, you can skip the first four steps. I've never had any problems shooting my Glock or blacked out. I shoot with my right hand and use my left for support and accuracy. My weapon is not my only means of defense. I also compete in CrossFit competitions to ensure I have the strength to confront would-be attackers.

The Maxi speech was supposed to be a fun, inexpensive date night. We had dinner—Mack drank a couple pints of Black and Tan—and got to Red Plaza at 6:15 pm. It was cold that night, so Mack was wearing his black leather jacket and carried a tan scarf just in case. I brought my Glock to the event, but I always have it with me, as well as Mack's pepper spray for protection. But I had no intention of using these defensive weapons. I had no reason at all to think protesters would be there. Although I knew violent anarchists were planning to disrupt Inauguration Day events, this had nothing to do with the inauguration. When we arrived, I was concerned to discover a few dozen masked Antiac counterprotesters shouting slogans and shoving people who were trying to get into the building. I couldn't tell who their leader was. I grew fearful when

I saw what Antiac was up to, but Mack promised he'd protect us. Mack circulated through the crowd, making sure everyone was safe. He'd pat people on the back, give pep talks, and try to convince protesters to accept that Stack was now their president. The Maxi haters were visibly upset and didn't like Mack touching them. A few of them told Mack to step back and accused him of being drunk. Mack may have been buzzed, but mostly he was riding a high from the inauguration. Mack wasn't trying to start anything. He was merely engaging in free speech. At 6:45, Mack was attacked by a protester who didn't like what he had to say. They ended up wrestling and Mack hurt his ankle. I shouted for police. They eventually arrived but by that point, Mack's attacker had disappeared into the crowd. I realized we were on our own.

Later, we saw a teenager we had met, Ari, walk up to some masked anarchists to ask about their signs. They jumped Ari and smashed a glass ornament filled with blue paint in his face! It was terrifying. Once again, the police did nothing! Mack ran up and told Antiac to relax. I worried they might hit him too. I may have reached for my gun at this moment, but I wasn't going to shoot anyone! Mack knows I'm anxious, so he patted my shoulders and said to stop being emotional. He was still smiling and laughing, putting on a brave face so I'd calm down.

Everything changed after Ari was attacked. Red Plaza suddenly felt like a battlefield in a video game, only this was for real. I knew that if push came to shove, we'd have to be willing to act on our constitutional right to defend ourselves. More fights broke out all around us, but each one of them was broken up without serious injuries. People were policing themselves.

I didn't notice Jeremy Dane until the moment he attacked Mack. Coincidentally, the night before the speech, I had stumbled on Jeremy's Tweets promising that Antiac would disrupt Inauguration Day events **(Ex. A, #1–2)**. Those Tweets contributed to my fear of the counterprotesters who appeared in Red Plaza that night without warning. But I didn't make the connection between the Twitter account and the person attacking my husband until later when Mr. Dane's name was reported on Action 10 News.

I'll never forget the moment I almost lost Mack. Hundreds of additional anti-Stack marchers had just entered the square from another demonstration downtown. They surrounded us and made us feel outnumbered. Mack tried to break the tension by humorously chanting along with some Maxi supporters waving a Jorge the Toad flag. Just then, some masked protesters started shoving an older guy who I now know is named Dom Nelson. Mr. Nelson was bent over, and the protesters began kicking at his head. Mack said, "Let's get 'em," and shot the attackers with pepper spray.

Just then, Mr. Dane came charging at us. Even though he wasn't wearing a mask or waving a flag, I could tell that he was with Antiac because he was wearing black. He was maybe 6'3". Mack's only 5'7". Mr. Dane was foaming at the mouth. In **Exhibit J, #1**, you can see how Mr. Dane grabbed Mack from behind with his left hand and reached for the pepper spray with his right hand. I figured Mr. Dane was upset about Mack pepper spraying his friends. Mr. Dane knocked me out of the way, causing me to stumble five feet back and hit the ground. I'm only 5'3'', 135 pounds. My arm was black and blue for days, but the injury may have healed by the time I sought medical treatment. The medical records accurately show my visit to the doctor.

I heard Jeremy yell something to the effect of, "I'm gonna gut you!" In **Exhibit J, #1**, you can see how Mack then broke free, turned to the left, and tried to escape. You can see Mack grinning—that's him putting on a brave face for me. Jeremy charged at Mack again, as seen in **Exhibit J, #3**. I'm in the foreground of the photo wearing pigtails. Mr. Dane spun Mack around to face him and kicked Mack's ankle. Mr. Dane kept using his left hand to pull at Mack's right wrist in the direction of the angry mob of counter-protesters. Mack was not asking for anyone's help or using the pepper spray in his own defense, which would have been dangerous. But I feared Mack would be pulled into the crowd and mobbed like Ari was. There were people everywhere, pushing, screaming. A muscular guy was trying to pull Mr. Dane off Mack, but he could barely keep his grip.

Mack started waving his tan scarf with his left hand. I took it as a signal that Mack was in distress. I heard a woman scream, "He's got a knife!" That's when I saw a large knife in Mr. Dane's right hand. I forgot to mention the knife later when I turned myself in to the police. It was only after I saw the Action 10 News report about Mr. Dane carrying a large knife that I remembered he was armed. The knife's blade was six inches long and black. It was difficult to see against Mr. Dane's black jacket, but I got a glimpse from my angle. Mr. Dane didn't make any threatening motions with the knife or raise it up. I had no time to think or weigh my options. I knew if I didn't act, my husband would be killed. We'd never again kiss goodbye or say good night! There were no police close enough to save Mack. I didn't yell for Mr. Dane to stop. The crowd was too noisy for that. And Mr. Dane was too big to shove.

That's when I pulled out my gun. You can see me extending my left arm in **Exhibit K, #1 and #2**. But then I think I blacked out. I don't remember aiming, shooting, hearing a gunshot, or feeling a kick. When I came to, Mr. Dane was on the ground and my gun was in my left hand. The fact that the gun was in my non-shooting hand makes me think I was simply firing a warning shot and not aiming at Mr. Dane. If I did aim at him, it was to save my husband's life.

I holstered my gun and desperately looked for Mack. I turned around and saw him behind me. It was like a white light was coming down and illuminating my darling Mack. I gave him the biggest hug. He whispered, "We need to escape," and he escorted us out of the square past several officers. I didn't stop to report anything because, at the time, I hadn't realized I fired my gun. Mack took us to the bus stop and told me to play Pokémon on my phone, which I did. Mack got us onto the first bus that came. He accidently left a yellow hat he'd found on the bus bench. Even though Mack rides the bus every day, we ended up on the wrong route. Once we realized our mistake, we rode a couple more miles and then switched buses.

At about 9:15, I was on the bus trying to piece together what happened. That's when I realized what must've happened and told Mack, "I think I shot that guy trying to gut you with the knife." Mack was talking to someone on the Facebook Messenger app on his phone. He looked up and said not to worry and to keep playing Pokémon. Mack wanted to first check my gun to confirm that it'd been fired. If we'd known about the news reports about a shooting, we would've immediately gone to the police. We got to our apartment at 9:45. It was then that Mack saw the casing in my gun and knew it had really happened. Mack and I broke down the sequence of the night's events and confirmed this was an act of self-defense. We immediately went to the station and turned over our weapons because we wanted to be as forthcoming as possible. I never asked police about Mr. Dane's condition, but I'm glad he survived.

MACK HODGMAN TESTIMONY[4]

My name is Mack Hodgman, and I'm twenty-three years old. I was born on a military base in Oahu and raised in a rural part of the island. I met my wife, Emily, in middle school. We began dating our freshman year. She's my Disney princess, and I would do anything for her. Emily moved in with my family at seventeen because of problems at home. When we graduated high school, we briefly worked as TSA screeners. But island living is so expensive that we couldn't make ends meet. So we moved to Nita City. I went to work installing floors, but I lost that job when the economy tanked and home construction dried up. Since then, I've been on unemployment and making plans to enroll in college. I'd like to become a doctor or nurse and help people. Emily was gonna stay home and raise the kids we'd like to have. But now, Emily's facing up to fifteen years in prison. If she's convicted, our dreams will be crushed.

I gave my wife her first gun, the Glock, and taught her to shoot. Emily's not as experienced as me and doesn't go to the range very often. I've never seen her misfire or black out when shooting. As for me, I've got 20/20 vision, so I'm a pretty good shot. A few years ago, Emily and I witnessed a police shooting, and the experience left Emily deeply shaken. She resolved to always have a firearm within reach for protection. She got her concealed pistol license and began consuming countless self-defense books and videos and socializing with other concealed-carry enthusiasts. I sometimes wonder if Emily lets her fear of being victimized get the best of her. She moves through the world like there's danger around every corner, with her gun serving as a security blanket. Still, despite her heightened sense of alertness, she's never used her gun irresponsibly.

We share many other hobbies, like flying kites, roller skating, and gaming. I'm shy and don't have a lot of guy friends. So gaming has allowed me to meet people like us. Our favorite table-top game is *Kings of the Dark Ages*. We paint our own figurines and enact epic battles. I'm "DoeNut the Defender," a warrior orc. Emily is "Sandra the Slayer," my warrior queen! We also play tons of video games, like *Space Warrior* and *Smash Bash 2000*, and first-person shooter games. My mom says I'm too engrossed in my games and can't separate fiction from reality. But that's silly. I want to be a doctor to help people. I would never hurt anyone.

I've never been political and, if anything, consider myself moderate. A few years ago, YouTube began turning us on to alternative voices like Maxi and The Upright Men. While I may have reposted the occasional Upright Men meme—known as a "Man-meme"—I've never been to a rally, participated in initiation, or intentionally worn their black and tan colors. Emily doesn't usually wear a ponytail like the Upright Women do. In the past, I may have acted like I belonged to the Upright Man online. But offline, I am no more a streetfighter than I am an orc. I will only use force to defend myself or others. Upright Men wasn't labeled an extremist group by the FBI until recently. I never would've reposted their stuff had I known they were a hate group.

---

4. The transcript of the witness's testimony at a preliminary hearing one week before trial was excerpted so that only the witness's answers are reprinted here. Assume that this is a true and accurate rendering of Mack Hodgman's answers under oath.

Exhibit C #1–3 are true and correct copies of my group conversation with Emily and Brendan on Facebook. The timestamps appear to be accurate. I feel ashamed of those messages and wish to apologize if anyone was offended. That was not my intent. But you have to understand, that's just how gamers talk in private. My messages with Brendan were just to impress him. I was just joking when I said the thing about getting into a "melee." I wasn't promoting actual aggression. The song "One Day More" is about bloodshed in the streets of Paris in the musical *Les Misérables*. How can I be an Upright Man if I like musical theater? Brendan was clearly excited about the inauguration of the man we loved so much. "Kill Them All" is from the movie *Starship Troopers*. This wasn't about violence. It was bravado and excitement for Stack. I assumed Emily would carry, but we didn't discuss it. "Veni vidi vici" means "I came, I saw, I conquered." I didn't open the Tucker McAdams link because my phone won't play videos. So I haven't a clue what it shows. Back then, I knew Tucker was the founder of Entice Media, but I didn't know he was affiliated with The Upright Men.

The night of the event, Emily and I had dinner, and we both drank a Black and Tan. Maybe I had two or three. I needed some liquid courage to stand up to Antiac. I was bundled for the cold in my black leather jacket and my tan scarf poking out of the pocket so I could grab it easily with my mittens. I was also carrying a Karambit knife **(Ex. L)** on my right waistband. The knife was a present from Emily. We'd seen it in the Strike Force video game, and I liked the cool "swooshing" sound effect it made in the game. The knife has a neat quick-draw ring and a curved, black blade that makes it difficult for an opponent to dislodge during a fight.

We arrived in Red Plaza at 6:30 and noticed Antiac blocking the venue. My wife looked uneasy and suggested we leave for our own safety. I told her I was armed and could protect the two of us. We were in high spirits because Stack was taking back America. At 6:45, we walked up to the front of Blaine Hall to investigate why the line to get in wasn't moving. It was so packed that I had to gently tap people on the back to move through the crowds. I tried to reason with a few protesters by suggesting they accept Stack was their president now too. I probably tossed around names like "snowflake" and "socialist." My words were intended to provoke a discussion. I wasn't trying to start an actual fight. One protester who objected to my patting his back pushed me and called me a fascist. I punched back in self-defense. We ended up wrestling and kicking each other's legs **(Ex. F)**. This happened near the park bench in the Diagram **(Ex. R)**, with the police looking on. I lost my red TBA ("Take Back America") hat in the scuffle but later replaced it with a yellow hat I discovered on the ground. I spoke to the police, but they did nothing to catch my attacker. I knew we'd have to defend ourselves.

At 7:45, a young Maxi fan named Ari approached some anarchists and asked about their signs. One of them yelled "fascist thief!" and hit Ari with a glass Christmas ornament. It was terrifying—it felt like an attack on a fellow Battle Brother. I ran up to the anarchists with my arms outstretched and tried to deescalate the conflict **(Ex. G, #1)**. Emily came up behind me and reached beneath her jacket for her gun **(Ex. G, #2)**. But by that point things had already calmed down considerably. So I patted my wife's shoulders and told her she needed to relax and not to shoot anyone. But that was just a turn of phrase. I didn't really think she'd start shooting. I then saw a guy in a TBA hat punching his fist into his palm like he wanted revenge for Ari. I yelled at him that "They have to start it" **(Ex. H)**. All I meant was the police wouldn't let us in to see Maxi if we were the ones starting fights instead of ending them. I'm sorry if anyone misconstrued my words as promoting violence.

I will never forget how the night ended. A couple hundred angry anti-Stack protesters from a downtown demonstration marched into the square from the south. By then, the ranks of Maxi supporters had thinned out considerably, and we were outnumbered and increasingly surrounded by counterprotesters. I tried to lighten the mood by joining in a chant of "Jorge!" in the direction of the protesters as someone waved a Jorge the Toad banner. I don't know who Jorge is, he just seemed like a funny cartoon character. In **Exhibit I #1**, I'm wearing a yellow hat on the right side of the frame. **Exhibit I #2** shows Jeremy Dane walking in front of us raising devil horns with his empty hands. Next, I saw several masked protesters roughing up the man who's been identified in the media as Dom Nelson. They were kicking at his head as he crouched over, which is a highly dangerous position to be in. I knew I needed to step up and protect him against Antiac. So I removed a pepper spray gun I had with me and shot two bursts of spray at Mr. Nelson's attackers. Unfortunately, I think Mr. Nelson also got some in his eyes.

Next thing I know, Dane comes charging up and grabs me from behind and starts reaching for my right hand. He screamed something to the effect of, "Why'd you do that, fascist? I'm gonna get you!" I broke free, spun around, and took several steps away to escape. While I had my back turned, I made sure I still had a firm grip on the pepper spray. He grabbed me, spun me back around to face him and kicked hard at my ankle and broke it. I screamed in pain. I didn't call for help because I thought I could fend for myself. I desperately waved the scarf, not as a signal to anyone, but in hopes of distracting Dane **(Ex. K, #1)**.

Exhibit K, #2 captures the very end of the fight, as I try to run away. I promise you, the black ring that's visible around my index finger is the pepper spray—not the quick-draw ring of my knife. Emily is behind my left shoulder with her left arm lifted. I could see she was holding her Glock. I believe this is the moment she fires. There was so much jostling that it probably made it difficult to aim. In this photograph, it looks like someone's got a grip on Jeremy's arm as he's pulled away. Just then, I heard a loud pop that I assumed was tear gas. I looked up, and Dane was gone. People were shouting, "They shot him!" But I assumed they were referring to the tear gas. I had no idea there'd been a shooting.

My wife was frantic. I gave her a hug and she whispered, "We need to escape," meaning we had to escape further Antiac violence. I walked Emily to the bus stop, sat her down, and suggested she play Pokémon on her phone. I ditched the yellow hat so we wouldn't stand out and get attacked again. In my race to escape, we accidently boarded the wrong bus. Even after discovering our mistake, we rode several more miles to get as far away from campus as possible before finally boarding the correct bus. On that second bus, Emily looked up from her phone and said, "I think I shot that guy because he was trying to gut you." I could see on my phone that it was about 9:30 pm when she said this. I had trouble believing there'd been a shooting.

At that point, I didn't even know it was on the news yet or that police were looking for us. Had I known, I would've immediately gotten off the bus and turned ourselves in. I told my wife to keep playing her game.

When we got home around 9:50, I checked Emily's Glock and saw the spent casing in the ejection port. That's when I knew it was real. I put the gun, my knife, and pepper spray in an American Girl shopping bag and drove us to the station to turn ourselves in. We walked into the station with our hands up. I said, "we're here to report a self-defense shooting" and Emily nodded in agreement. Before I was taken into custody, neither of us told police who pulled the trigger or mentioned what led to the shooting. We thought it best to talk to a lawyer first.

Three days later, I went to the hospital and told the doctor about Dane kicking my foot and twisting my wrist. I went back on March 3 because I was suffering excruciating pain and wanted to document my injuries. I again told the doctors exactly what Dane did, but it's possible medical personnel didn't write down verbatim what I told them.

We've avoided news coverage of the incident. I do remember, though, in late January YR-3, we were painting figurines when an Action 10 News report came on the TV about how knives and brass knuckles had been located on Dane's person. I personally don't remember seeing a knife in Dane's hand. Emily was silent, but she was watching the report intently.

ARI SINCLAIR TESTIMONY[5]

My name is Ari Sinclair. I am a resident of Evergreen, just north of Nita City. After graduating from Mariner High School, I went to work at Cameron's Sporting Goods so I could save enough money to go to flight school and become a commercial pilot.

In my free time, I enjoy watching YouTube videos. I don't drink or smoke, so I get my kicks from provocative YouTubers like Maxi Rossi. I appreciate Mr. Rossi for his astute comedic observations at the expense of politicians and social justice warriors. But like the late, great George Carlin, Mr. Rossi goes right up to the line. I also enjoy watching videos that cast historical events in a new light. I am a conspiracy enthusiast. For instance, did you know the moon landing was actually broadcast from a Hollywood sound stage? Seriously, it was carried out by a cabal of far-left government insiders trying to polish JFK's legacy. I believe it was a hoax, even if I can't prove it.

My dad agreed to take me to Maxi's speech to celebrate my eighteenth birthday. I figured we'd have a few laughs and head home. Goodness was I wrong! We arrived at 6 pm. I was wearing my red TBA hat and a cross on the outside of my sweatshirt. We didn't arm ourselves because there was no reason to carry a weapon to a political event. When we first arrived, there were some peaceful protesters dancing with feathers and smoking marijuana cigarettes. Cops stood behind some barricades at the top of the steps leading into Blaine Hall. My dad and I milled about with other Maxi fans as we waited to get in **(Ex. D)**.

At about 6:20 pm, a few dozen Antiac activists marched into Red Plaza **(Ex. E)**. They wore ski masks and bandanas, waved black-and-red flags, and chanted "No Stack, No Way, No Fascist USA." They briefly circled us before marching up to the front of Blaine Hall to form a human blockade **(Ex. R)**. Antiac tormented and taunted us by throwing eggs, glass bottles, and ugly words in our direction. They even chiseled red bricks out of the ground and hurled them in our direction. Several Maxi supporters tried to storm the building but were violently shoved back by Antiac. The police were no help because they were stationed behind the wall of Antiac idiots. We were like sitting ducks and forced to fend for ourselves.

Throughout the night, I kept an eye on a person who I've come to believe was Antiac's leader. He was 5'11", white, early 40s, shaved head, wearing a black sweatshirt or jacket, black running shoes, and a red bandana that covered the lower half of his face. I can't say for sure, but this person closely resembled the photos I've seen of Jeremy Dane on the news website BiteBack. com. The Antiac leader kept rallying his supporters by yelling things like, "Don't stop going after fascists!" and "shut it down!" He was trying to incite a riot and then blame it on us. When a Maxi supporter politely suggested he take a deep breath, the leader kicked at him and stomped away in a huff. At one point, I saw the Antiac leader whispering into his cell phone as he plotted

---

5. The transcript of the witness's testimony at a preliminary hearing one week before trial was excerpted so that only the witness's answers are reprinted here. Assume that this is a true and accurate rendering of the witness's answers under oath.

next steps. At that exact moment, I saw two other Antiac protesters also on their cell phones. I even saw a police officer speaking into his radio. And that's when I put the pieces together and realized Antiac was conspiring with the police to commit violence against us! From that point on, I knew the police would not protect us. I watched as the Antiac leader stuffed his phone into the pocket of his black jacket. I could tell trouble was brewing and stayed close to my dad for protection.

I met Mr. and Mrs. Hodgman in line. Mr. Hodgman was wearing a red TBA hat and a black jacket with a tan winter scarf sticking out of the pocket. Mrs. Hodgman wore pigtails and a big coat. Neither of them concealed their faces or identified as members of The Upright Men. Mr. Hodgman was outgoing and funny, though I could smell alcohol on his breath. He was shouting profanities at the protesters—calling them socialists and snowflakes and informing them that Stack was their president now, too. I enjoyed speaking to Mrs. Hodgman about politics and her hobby of competing in CrossFit strength competitions. She said Mr. Hodgman enjoys using good-natured humor to "trigger the libs" but that they both were willing to "go to battle" in defense of this country if the situation presented itself.

Eventually, the police gave Antiac exactly what they wanted and closed down the event. At that point, Mr. Hodgman began politely working his way through the crowds and approaching clusters of Antiac protesters. Mrs. Hodgman followed after him, nervously clinging to the back of his belt or his shoulder. Around 6:45 pm, I heard a protester yell, "Back up, fascist!" and looked over and saw Mr. Hodgman wrestling someone **(Ex. F)**. Mrs. Hodgman was frantically shouting for the police. But by the time an officer made it through the dense crowd, people had pulled them apart. That's how all the fights ended that night. No one ever got hurt. Mr. Hodgman went around saying he'd won the fight because liberals don't bench. I noticed he was walking with a limp after the fight. Mrs. Hodgman told me her husband "doesn't start fights, he ends them." They didn't seem to mind the aggression and were having a good time.

That changed after I was attacked. You see, I started to get bored, so around 7:45 pm, I followed Mr. Hodgman's example and approached some Antiac members gathered near the park bench **(Ex. R)** in hopes of having a constructive conversation about our differences. I reached out to grab one of their signs in hopes of getting a closer look at what it said. That's when one of them called me a "fascist thief," pulled me into their mob, and jumped me. They ripped off my cross, broke my nose, and shattered a paint-filled ornament in my face. You can see the blue paint on my face in **Exhibit G, #2**, taken immediately after the attack. Mrs. Hodgman yelled for the police, but none came. The Antiac leader I had seen was not among my attackers.

As things calmed down, Mr. Hodgman ran up and confronted my attackers. You can see him extending his arms in **Exhibit G, #1**. I believe he was playing peacemaker by putting himself between me and Antiac. In the photo, I'm behind him in a brown vest. That's my dad with his hand on my back. Mrs. Hodgman was trembling and tearful. You can see her with her hand beneath the back of her jacket, but I never saw a weapon. Mr. Hodgman went up to a guy in a red TBA hat who was vengefully pounding his fist into his hand as he glared at Antiac **(Ex. H)**.

Mr. Hodgman encouraged him to exercise restraint, telling the guy, "They have to start it" referring to Antiac. Mrs. Hodgman nodded her head in agreement.

Mr. Hodgman gave me a bear hug, called me his "Battle Brother," and said the blood and paint on my face showed I was fighting for the red, white, and blue. Mrs. Hodgman said, "You'll see, there's gonna be hell to pay for what they did to you" and called out for the police a second time, but none came. A few minutes later, I saw Mrs. Hodgman hand her husband a dark rectangular object that I assumed was a flask. Mr. Hodgman intently scanned the crowd of Antiac protesters as he pensively tapped the flask against his right thigh. Mr. Hodgman told his wife to "wait for the signal." Mrs. Hodgman caught me looking at her husband, pressed her index finger to her lips, and said, "Shh." I figured they wanted to keep their booze a secret.

We did not report the assault on me to the police because it would've been dangerous to get through the Antiac mob to reach the officers behind the barricades. Instead, we left Red Plaza at around 8 pm. We didn't encounter any difficulty safely leaving the square. On the way to our car, we overheard firefighters say police were ignoring all the people getting hit with paint-filled ornaments. At 9:20, I saw a breaking news alert stating that university police were looking for a short, pudgy man in a black leather jacket. That description matched Mr. Hodgman.

At the emergency room, a nurse removed glass from my hair. I was diagnosed with a broken nose and a concussion. Since the concussion, I've experienced loss of concentration and memory. I have trouble remembering names and faces. And I'm sensitive to noise and lights.

On January 22, YR-3, I emailed Lt. Garcia about what I had witnessed. He wrote me back saying he had all he needed to close the case and didn't need to speak with me because I didn't see the shooting. When I wrote that the gunshot victim got what he deserved, I was referring to his attack on Mr. Hodgman, not his politics.

Earlier this year, I was convicted of petty theft after some Antiac members accused me of stealing their signs and backpacks in Red Plaza. It was a total lie—I had been picking up their litter. But Antiac threatened the DA that if she did not bring charges against me, they would mobilize social justice warriors to elect someone new. There was rampant lawlessness on both sides that night. But apparently the government is only interested in going after Stack supporters. I agreed to plead guilty in order to receive a lighter sentence.

EXPERT REPORTS

Report of Pat Sadie, PhD

University of Nita Professor

January 1, YR-0

Background

I am a part-time lecturer in video game culture and political sociology in the Comparative History of Ideas Program at the University of Nita. I received my BA in English literature and my master's in political sociology from Nita State University in YR-5. I am working towards my PhD in English, expected next year. I am the founder of the Critical Video Gaming Program, an interdisciplinary program at the University of Nita that facilitates the critical study of computer and social games. My focus is learning how games affect human interactions and perceptions for the 60 million Americans who play them. My PhD work includes the study of online political subcultures, disinformation campaigns, and the connection between video game culture and political extremism.

I offered to work on this case after reading about the incident in the *Nita Times*. I have known Emily Hodgman for seven years through our involvement in the tabletop gaming community. In YR-4, I competed against Ms. Hodgman in a "Warrior Quest" game tournament. I was disqualified after Ms. Hodgman and her partner, Brendan Kellogg, wrongly accused me of microwaving my game dice to alter their weight distribution, causing them to land more often on the side favorable to me. I was denied a title that rightfully belonged to me. I was suspended from competition for five years. I am appealing the suspension and anticipate my gaming rights will be reinstated fully. I hold no ill will towards Ms. Hodgman, and this in no way invalidates my research. In fact, the episode represented a remarkable one-off in my dealings with Ms. Hodgman, as she has a reputation in the gamer community for integrity and level-headedness. I have never known her to use hate speech or advocate violence, though it has been a few years since I competed against her.

In preparing this report, I relied on information the prosecutor provided to me, as well as the social media activity of Emily and Mack Hodgman and Jeremy Dane. I did not interview Ms. Hodgman due to her right to remain silent. I also did not request a copy of Ms. Hodgman's police interview to review because I understand her statement is not admissible in the prosecution's case in chief. Photographs and witness statements, which could shed some light on the events of January 20, were not provided.

I understand from the prosecution that Ms. Hodgman claims she pointed her gun at the defenseless and unarmed victim to protect her husband. In order to evaluate this claim, the jury must understand Ms. Hodgman's far-right affiliations. I offer no opinion as to whether Ms. Hodgman has a propensity to commit violence. Rather, this subject matter is relevant to Ms. Hodgman's motives and to rebut the claim that the shooting was an accident or in defense of another. This subject is sufficiently beyond common understanding that I believe my expertise would assist the trier of fact in evaluating Ms. Hodgman's testimony.

Online Radicalization

Multiplayer video games—and their associated chatroom and livestream features—are increasingly fertile ground for far-right radicalization on the internet. Seemingly casual conversations with a stranger about race or economics can quickly lead a gamer down a rabbit hole of increasingly hateful rhetoric, memes, and videos designed to normalize nationalist ideology. One study found that a quarter of gamers had been exposed to in-game discussions about the "superiority of whites." Often young, disaffected, and male, gamers are particularly susceptible to messages that play on their cultural and economic insecurities.

YouTube is another common avenue into the world of extremism. Known as "the Great Radicalizer," YouTube's algorithm for recommending videos uses artificial intelligence to push increasingly outrageous content on viewers. A gamer might start off watching a livestream by one of his favorite gamers when suddenly YouTube recommends an attention-grabbing video by an alt-right influencer. Viewers become trapped in a "filter bubble" that feeds and reinforces extreme views, contributing to the rise and unification of the far-right. Far-right activists have learned to exploit the algorithm to draw new viewers. Once radicalized, a young person can move on to private social media groups and message boards where extremist views and conspiracy theories are spread through memes, coded language, and inside jokes.

Maximus Rossi and The Upright Men

I am not surprised that Mack and Emily Hodgman attended the event on January 20. The Hodgmans fit the profile of young, disaffected gamers who are easily seduced by the far right. Maxi Rossi is a far-right YouTuber who came to attention through his videos promoting an online harassment campaign that targeted feminist critics of the male-dominated gaming industry.

Rossi is closely aligned with The Upright Men ("TUM"), a nationalist street gang. Part fraternity, part fight club, TUM supported Daniel Stack's Take Back America presidential campaign. They deplore "social justice warriors" and what they call "P.C. culture." Membership is divided into four closely-guarded ranks. Level one is achieved when the member publicly states, "I am a proud Upright Man, and I refuse to apologize for Western civilization." Level two requires enduring a beating by other members while shouting out quotes from 80s films. Level three entails getting a large TUM tattoo on the forearm. And level four requires fighting a political opponent. TUM members flaunt their affiliation by wearing western shirts with pearl snaps or wearing black and tan, the colors of their favorite drink.

TUM's modus operandi is to engage in violence with far-left groups under the guise of self-defense. Members act in a provocative manner that all but guarantees violence and view the slightest aggression as justification for force. Their founder, Tucker McAdams, once urged new initiates to "find Antiac, beat Antiac." McAdams later backpedaled by claiming, "The Upright Men don't start fights, we finish them." Members are careful to only carry weapons that can easy be categorized as "defensive," such as pepper spray and mace, so as to avoid arrest. I have studied more than thirty Upright Men street brawls, and I am not aware of a single instance in which a gun was used.

Before an event, TUM uses private online messages to plot tactics and exchange memes, music, and videos celebrating violence. For instance, the night before the January 20 inauguration, a video of McAdams punching an Antiac counterprotester outside the so-called Chauvinist Ball went viral on YouTube. After the event, TUM released a "clarifying statement" indicating that "violence is not a condition precedent to receiving the fourth level of membership."

Last month, the FBI labeled TUM a domestic terrorist group and warned of the potential for violence on college campuses. However, following unprecedent intervention by President Stack, the FBI reversed itself and said the agency was merely describing the threat posed by some individual members and that the group was by and large peaceful. Far right media seized on the reversal to argue that TUM is neither a gang nor violent and was instead invented to "troll" liberals.

The Upright Girls is a much smaller spinoff group consisting of women in a relationship with an Upright Man. Upright Girls are purportedly told to wear their hair in ponytails at Upright Men events and to "stand by your man," by backing up Upright Men in the streets and taking care of the family at home. When an Upright Man finds himself in trouble during a fight, he will give a sign to his female counterpart to come assist him. It could be as simple as yelling out a code word or waving something around. Upright Girls show their adulation for their men by posting "proud of my man" on social media. That said, beyond a smattering of Upright Girls social media accounts, there is little evidence that there is much of an organization to speak of. The only known instance of violence involving an Upright Girl came in YR-0 when a Nita state trooper was fired after she video-recorded her boyfriend beating an Antiac activist.

The Hodgmans' Facebook messages are sprinkled with references to video games and the extreme right. The term "Battle Brother" refers to militia members who defend the galaxy from alien invaders in the game *Space Warrior*. Gamers use the term to show comradery. "Melee" is a term of art used in *Dragons and Slayers* and *Smash Bash 2000*. Melee refers to a category of disorganized combat between video game characters in close quarters using a "melee weapon" such as a sword, dagger, or club. In contrast, a "ranged weapon" is one that launches projectiles at a distant target, including javelins, slingshots, and firearms. Here, Mack engaged in melee combat when he wrestled a counterprotester. However, when he and Emily used their pepper spray and handgun, they were deploying *ranged* weapons, albeit at very close range.

The Hodgmans' Facebook messages also use far-right language (**Ex. C, #1–3**). "Snowflake" is meant to mock hypersensitive political opponents, particularly on the left. The expression "*deus vult*" ("God wills it") is a rallying cry used by Christian knights during the Crusades. Extremist groups appropriated the expression in their memes. Jorge the Toad is a cartoon character also co-opted by extremists to express hate while preserving plausible deniability.

Ms. Hodgman's Facebook profile contains numerous references to far-right groups and influences, including the extremist "news" website BiteBack and The Upright Girls itself (**Ex. B**). Of course, merely "liking" an organization on social media is a far cry from enlistment. I cannot definitively say that Ms. Hodgman is an Upright Girl, to the extent the group actually exists, or testify to what is in her mind or heart. Had the police done a thorough investigation by obtaining Ms. Hodgman's private Facebook activity, as opposed to merely that of her husband, I could make a more definitive conclusion about her political allegiance. Nevertheless, Ms. Hodgman's activities are certainly consistent with support for TUM and its female counterpart.

The Anti-Authoritarian Coalition ("Antiac") is TUM's political rival. Antiac is a loose, secretive affiliation of anarchists and other radicals who use violence and intimidation in their effort to remove authoritarianism from the figurative and literal public square. They teach that physical confrontations and intimidation are justified to prevent fascist attacks on marginalized communities. Militant Antiac protesters have repeatedly clashed with right-wing attendees and the occasional journalist at political events. Because members dress in all black and conceal their identities with hoodies and ski masks, it can be difficult to distinguish one from another. Jeremy Dane's Twitter messages suggest he is sympathetic with Antiac's cause. But like Ms. Hodgman, I cannot fully understand his political leanings, or speak to his intentions on January 20, because police failed to obtain a warrant for his Twitter direct messages.

I believe the Hodgmans have internalized a form of political and cultural tribalism that fuels distrust and animosity towards leftist groups like Antiac. This hostility causes them to perceive threats, both real and imagined, to their culture, economic security, and personal safety. This worldview fuels hypervigilance and, at its most extreme, the embrace of political violence. The shooting was neither an accident nor an act done to defend her husband. Rather, I believe the Hodgmans intentionally created the circumstances that allowed Mack to fight, and Emily to shoot, a political enemy under the guise of self-defense.

Compensation

I have devoted twelve hours to this case at a rate of $300 per hour. My rate for trial testimony is $500 per hour. I plan on writing an article in the *Journal of Social Media* about this incident. The publication, my first, will put me on a tenure track.

Brighton Stevens, PhD
Lethal Force Institute

Client: Emily Hodgman

Case: State of Nita v. Emily Hodgman

Date of Report: February 25, YR-1

Background

I am a licensed forensic psychologist specializing in police and public safety psychology. After earning a bachelor's degree in criminal justice, I joined the City of Nita Police Department as a commissioned officer. I ran the department's gun range and taught marksmanship, reactive shooting, and basic forensic ballistics investigations at the police academy.

After ten years, I wanted to better understand the role of stress during police work. I left the force and re-enrolled in school, earning a master's degree and PhD in clinical psychology. I founded the Lethal Force Institute (LFI), which studies the body's arousal in response to threats. I am the lead author of a study published in the *Journal of Forensic Sciences* that analyzed police officers' physiological responses during dispatch calls.

While I also offer my services to the government, the prosecution has not yet hired me because they maintain their own experts through the state Crime Lab. My law enforcement background demonstrates I approach cases in an unbiased and professional manner.

Materials Reviewed

On February 20, YR-1, I interviewed Emily Hodgman. The twenty-minute interview was not recorded, and I shredded my handwritten notes once I drafted this report. Mack Hodgman was present. Emily stated she was "on high alert," "jittery," and armed for her defense when she entered Red Plaza on January 20, YR-3, because she had seen Antiac postings on social media promoting violent disruption of Inauguration Day events using the #DisruptJ20 hashtag on social media.

Emily stated that a man resembling an Antiac activist she had seen online attacked her husband while raising a knife with a three-inch, silver-tipped blade in a menacing manner. Emily said the attack was "entirely unprovoked" and, at the time, she did not understand the reason the activist accosted her husband. The suddenness and randomness of the attack caused her heart to race and she experienced shortness of breath. Emily stated that she remembers firing the gun with her left hand, even though she normally shoots with her right hand and uses her left for support and accuracy, and she does not know the direction in which the gun was aimed.

After interviewing Emily, I visited the police station and examined weapons collected in this case and photos of the incident.

National Institute for Trial Advocacy 53

The Body's Response to Threats

Emily's actions must be understood in the context of the body's response to threats. This is an area of science about which most jurors lack understanding. The amygdala is the area of the brain that processes emotions. When a person senses danger, whether real or imagined, the amygdala interprets the images and sounds and sends a distress signal to the hypothalamus, the body's command center, leading to the production of adrenaline and other hormones. Adrenaline increases the heart rate, blood pressure, and breathing rate. It takes twenty to sixty minutes for the body to return to its pre-arousal states after a threat.

This so called "fight-or-flight" response is a survival mechanism enabling quick, automatic reactions with potentially little forethought. The level of danger that a person perceives influences their capacity for rational decision-making. The frontal lobes are where reasoning and decision-making occur. The lobes help us manage emotions and determine a logical response to danger. When a person encounters a low-level threat, the frontal lobes overcome the amygdala's fight-or-flight response and enable a reasoned reaction. But when a person senses a high-level threat, the amygdala acts quickly, inhibiting rational thought (**Ex. S**).

The acute stress response can also affect memory. Jurors and other lay people often believe that surprising and consequential events create a "flashbulb memory" in which the details of the incident can be accurately recalled. To the contrary, research shows stress causes inaccuracy of perception and subsequent distortion during recall.

Most jurors have also heard about purported feats of extreme strength during life-and-death situations, such as lifting a car off a baby. Research is inconclusive as to whether adrenaline actually increases strength in time of danger. What is clear, however, is that we experience a decrease in fine motor skills during high stress. My own peer-reviewed research found a statistically significant deterioration in shooting skills and accuracy among officers during high-risk encounters with armed individuals in motion versus low-risk conditions involving static or unarmed persons.

Weapons Examination

Inside the ejection port of Emily's 9 mm Glock, I located a spent 9 mm cartridge case that failed to eject (**Ex. M**). Lt. Garcia appears to have overlooked this critical piece of evidence when he failed to properly examine the gun in his rush to file charges.

The location of the spent cartridge case strongly indicates that the gun experienced a "stovepipe" malfunction when it was last fired. Improper holding technique, known as "limp wristing," is one cause of a stovepipe malfunction. When a semi-automatic pistol is fired, the energy that propels the bullet forward pushes the slide to the rear. However, when the user fails to hold the gun firm and straight, the gun can flip up during the recoil. This disrupts the gun's linear inertia and may interfere with the slide's movement, preventing the casing from ejecting. Emily's Glock was susceptible to this type of firing error due to its light-weight polymer frame. The Glock requires a rigid grip to ensure accuracy and prevent malfunction. A stovepiped gun cannot shoot again until the round is cleared. (A stovepipe malfunction can also result from mechanical failure, such as from a weak recoil spring, or defects in the ammunition. However, because I was not asked to test fire the weapon, and Lt. Garcia neglected to do so, I cannot definitively rule out a mechanical failure.)

I examined the cartridge case closer and determined it once carried a hollow-point bullet. When the hollow-point bullet met Mr. Dane's human tissue, its concave tip in all probability expanded like an umbrella. This occurs by design. The mushrooming of the bullet allows it to slow down upon impact and remain inside a person's body. The design of the bullet increases the amount of tissue crushed and shredded and typically causes significant impairment to the function of any body part or organ it hits. Hollow-point bullets are a safe, responsible ammunition in a self-defense situation or crowded environments. Unlike "range ammunition" such as full-metal jacket rounds, that can potentially blast straight through a target and hit the innocent, hollow-point bullets reduce the likelihood of collateral damage and require fewer bullets to incapacitate attackers.

Finally, I examined the Guardian Angel pepper spray and the knife. The pepper spray **(Ex. N)** releases two blasts of liquid spray that can cause severe burning, temporary blindness, and coughing. In the screen image seen in **Exhibit N**, Mr. Hodgman has the pepper spray in his right hand. Red lines show the white nozzles at the weapon's tip.

Interestingly, Mr. Hodgman appears to have a *second* device in his right hand near the tail end of the incident. A black ring is visible around his index finger. **(Ex. K, #2)**. This does not appear to be the pepper spray given the width of the ring and the absence of the white nozzles **(Ex. N)**. Although the ring appears consistent with the "quick-draw" ring on the Karambit knife **(Ex. L)**, Mr. Hodgman told me during my interview of his wife that he did not remove the knife from his pocket during the altercation. I have no reason to doubt his denial.

Analysis

Emily described experiencing symptoms on January 20, YR-3, that are consistent with a fight-or-flight response. She perceived an unprovoked attack on her husband by a member of Antiac, a group that Emily was preconditioned to believe was dangerous and who she had seen harass and assault attendees all evening. Her perception of a raised knife in Mr. Dane's hand sent her already elevated adrenaline into overdrive. This caused the increased heart rate, shallow breathing, and diminished motor control that she describes.

Because Emily arguably perceived a high-level threat, her frontal lobes were unable to override the amygdala's survival response. To the extent Emily shot Mr. Dane on purpose, her actions were driven by instinct, without the benefit of rational decision-making or the ability to weigh reasonable alternatives. To quote Justice Oliver Wendell Holmes, "Detached reflection cannot be demanded in the presence of an uplifted knife." On the illustrative exhibit **(Ex. S)**, Emily's stress response would be somewhere near the tip of the arrow.

My opinion might change under a different set of facts. For example, consider a hypothetical where Emily had grown accustomed to the violence that night, did not actually perceive a raised knife, and understood Mr. Dane to have innocent intentions in confronting her husband. In that scenario, Emily would have perceived a lower-level threat, and her frontal lobes would in theory enable a more reasoned reaction. Indeed, a reasonably prudent person faced with those circumstances might choose a different course than firing her gun. I did not receive or request a copy of Mr. Dane's statement to the police. Although his statement could help illuminate his intentions in raising his knife at Mr. Hodgman, ultimately it is Emily's perceptions of a threat that matter. Of course, information is only as good as its source.

Emily does not remember aiming the gun, and my examination of the evidence suggests she did not purposefully fire at Mr. Dane's stomach. The presence of the casing in the ejection port suggests Emily was limp-wristing the weapon due to poor motor control associated with the stressful event, her left-handed grip, and/or a lack of intentionality in her actions. The jostling of the crowd would have further impacted her grip and accuracy.

Based on all these factors, I believe that the gun was not intentionally shot in Mr. Dane's direction. Based on her decision to hold the gun with her nondominant left hand, thus forgoing the accuracy of her normal two-handed grip, Emily may have attempted to fire a warning shot at the ground but accidently hit Mr. Dane as the weapon recoiled upwards. Had Emily intended to cause great bodily harm to Mr. Dane, I believe she would have fired more than once.

The irony is that in firing the warning shot, Emily hit the one part of the body that students are taught to aim for in self-defense classes. In fact, the preeminent self-defense scholar Mark Arans writes in his book *Fatal Engagements* that one should aim for the middle part of the attacker's body because it is the biggest, easiest target and quickest way to neutralize a threat. Shooting at someone's feet or hands is reckless because bystanders could be injured.

Compensation

I charge a flat fee of $1,500 for initial case review and $200 per hour after that. I have billed 20 hours to date on this case. After reviewing a draft report, a client can decide whether to retain me for trial, whereupon I charge $600 per hour to testify, with a minimum of eight hours. I've testified for the defense fourteen times in criminal cases. In YR-1, I presented on "Successful Ballistic Defenses" for the Nita City Public Defender's Association.

MEDICAL REPORTS

 **Norwegian Medical Center**
Nita City

HODGMAN, MACK—H23456
Medical Record/Note
Visit Date: 23 January YR-3 @ 1900

Norwegian Emergency Department

HISTORY OF PRESENT ILLNESS
Patient reports that he was "goofing off" Friday night in Red Plaza when he got into a wrestling match with a protester. The protester tried to kick patient's legs out from beneath him. This injured his right/foot ankle. Initially able to place weight on foot and ankle. Had Fire evaluate. Has tried icing and ibuprofen. Also feels right wrist sprained from a second person attempting to grab something out of his hand. This second altercation made right foot pain even worse. Patient concerned won't be able to go to his martial arts class. Currently filing a claim. Does not get into details of altercations. Has not made police report.

CHIEF COMPLAINTS
Right foot pain, right ankle pain, swollen right wrist.

BODY SYSTEM REVIEW
General: No unexplained weight loss. No dizziness. No fatigue.
Skin: No rash, itching, or redness.
Ear/eyes/throat: No change in vision or hearing loss.
Cardiovascular: No chest pain.
Respiratory: No SOB. No wheezing or cough.
Musculoskeletal: No swollen joints. No leg cramps.
Psychiatric: No headaches. No anxiety or depression. No drug or alcohol use.

ALLERGIES
Peanuts. No known drug allergies.

SOCIAL HISTORY
Student. Married.

ORDERS
X-ray—right foot, ankle

ASSESSMENT
Avulsion fracture right ankle. Right foot and ankle swelling. Right wrist with swelling, tender to palpation.

TREATMENT
I discussed with patient the imaging findings, pointing out the issue of concern and the location of the fracture. Informed patient to ice, elevate, and use ACE compression. Ibuprofen and return if the pain increases.

Electronic Signature
Fletch, Chevy, Resident, Norwegian Medical Center

Norwegian Medical Center
Nita City

HODGMAN, MACK (8/19/87)—H23456
Medical Record/Note
Visit Date: 3 March YR-3 @ 1600

Follow-up Office Visit

Patient states desire to document injury. Reports mild, dull, throbbing pain related to fractured ankle. States that the injury was caused by protester kicking ankle during altercation. Patient presents today in regular shoe and crutches. Patient states swelling has gone down. Advised patient to continue to elevate foot and to use ACE wrap. Return in 3–4 weeks or sooner if pain increases.

Electronic Signature
Fletch, Chevy
Resident, Norwegian Medical Center

 **Norwegian Medical Center**
Nita City

HODGMAN, EMILY—H65436
Medical Record/Note
Visit Date: 23 January YR-3 @ 1915

Norwegian Emergency Department

HISTORY OF PRESENT ILLNESS

Patient is a 22 yo female who presents for right hip and shoulder pain. Patient states on 1/20, she was tackled by a stranger who was seeking to restrain the person in front of her. This knocked her to the side with contact to her right side. Denies LOC. She did not fall to the ground. Starting two days later, she began experiencing pain on right side. Patient describes other bodily pain related to workout she had prior to altercation on 1/20. Hip pain intensity is 1 out of 10 when walking. Shoulder pain 1/10.

CHIEF COMPLAINTS: Right hip pain, right shoulder pain

BODY SYSTEM REVIEW

General: Unremarkable. Generally healthy.
Skin: No rash, itching, or redness.
Ear/eyes/throat: No change in vision or hearing loss.
Cardiovascular: No chest pain.
Respiratory: No SOB. No wheezing or cough.
Musculoskelatal: No swollen joints. No leg cramps. No restless leg.
Psychiatric: No headaches. No anxiety or depression. No drug or alcohol use.

SOCIAL HISTORY

Banker. Married

ASSESSMENT: No swelling or bruising detected on shoulder or hip. Patient is improving. Low pain. No distress. Pleasant female. Minor bruising on left side of body, which patient states she received in her CrossFit class.

TREATMENT: I discussed with the patient that her hip and shoulder appear to be healing well and should be fully recovered 2–4 weeks. Return for worsening pain.

Electronic Signature
Fletch, Chevy
Resident, Norwegian Medical Center

EXHIBITS

Electronic exhibits can be found at the following website:
http://bit.ly/1P20Jea
Password: Hodgman1

Jeremy Dane's Twitter Postings

Jeremy Dane @JDane ·
🔁 Jeremy Dane retweeted

HopSkip @Hopskip · 5:15 pm 19 Jan Yr-3

My sign tomorrow
#StopMaxie #DisruptJ20

🔁 24   ♡ 96

Jeremy Dane @JDane · 7:00 pm 19 Jan Yr-3

Why is #UniversityOfNita allowing a transphobic racist to speak on campus? We intend on shutting it down! #DisruptJ20

🔁 3   ♡ 10

Jeremy Dane @JDane · 8:20 pm 19 Jan Yr-3

Everybody get ready...
Ten Reasons to Go Hard on January 20
#DisruptJ20

🔁 7   ♡ 20

Jeremy Dane @JDane · 11:15 am 20 Jan Yr-3

Never stop going after fascists

🔁 8   ♡ 5

Jeremy Dane @JDane · 11:16 am 20 Jan Yr-3

Destroying bourgeois property is hella good praxis #DisruptJ20

🔁 10   ♡

Jeremy Dane @JDane · 11:26 am 20 Jan Yr-3

This morning anti-authoritarian patriots are defying the security state and smashing banks, starbucks, limousines and attacking the police. Let's burn it all down.
#DisruptJ20 #TurnBackStack

🔁 11   ♡ 25

Jeremy Dane @JDane · 1:15 pm 20 Jan Yr-3

BREAKING: DC Police teargas anti-Stack protesters outside Upright Men event
#TurnBackStack

🔁 5   ♡ 18

Jeremy Dane @JDane · 1:16 pm 20 Jan Yr-3

#DisruptJ20 legal support hotline: 422-4663

🔁 6   ♡ 18

Jeremy Dane @JDane · 1:19 am 20 Mar Yr-0

It's time to talk about restorative justice

🔁 6   ♡ 18

Jeremy Dane @JDane · 1:20 am 20 Mar Yr-0

I was disempowered by a bullet... and am disempowered again when the government can't give me the justice I want

🔁 9   ♡ 30

Exhibit B

"About" Page from Emily Hodgman's Facebook Account

Take Back America!

#Stand with Turner

Emily Hodgman
(Sandra the Slayer)

Home   About   Posts   Friends   Photos   Videos

Groups

Pen and Paper Gaming Association
Dragons and Slayers
Space Warrior Gamers
Worthington Anime Goods Exchange
University of Worthington Social Gaming
The Upright Girls
GamerGate and ComicsGate Discussion
Tabletop Fantasies
CrossFit Competition
BoardGameGeek

Likes

Kite flying
American Girl
Roller skating
The Upright Girls
Maxi Rossi
BiteBack.com
National Rifle Association
Smash Bash 2000
Video Games Talk on Reddit
Take Back America
Daniel Turner

Exhibit C #1–2

Facebook Messenger Chat from Mack Hodgman's Account

Facebook Business Records
Response to Warrant No. YR-3-00278
Account: Mack Hodgman

National Institute for Trial Advocacy

Facebook Business Records
Response to Warrant No. YR-3-00278
Account: Mack Hodgman

Group chat 📞 📹 ⓘ

01-19-YR-3 7:35 pm

lol, that's us tomorrow night

01-19-YR-3 7:36 pm

Emily Hodgman
Proud of my man... Mack's going for Level Four... No Antiac jerks are gonna silence us.

01-19-YR-3 7:37 pm

Brendan Kellog
GET EM.... I'll be strapped. Extra mag and my ankle gun on. I hear the city's gonna be a war zone tomorrow.

01-19-YR-3 7:38 pm

I honestly can't wait

01-20-YR-3 1:00 pm

Brendan Kellog
[BiteBack News: Daniel Stack's Inauguration Live Stream]. It's starting!!! Wont lie... a tear or two are slipping out... we live in the best time, beside the revolutionary war... we're the president now... god I could die happy... Message me after Maxi! Go GET EM!

01-20-YR-3 6:45 pm

Hey Maxi, im outside your event. I got sucker punched and kicked in the leg just now. someone jacked my #TBA hat... Anyway for me to get a replacement signed by you?

01-20-YR-3 9:25 pm

Brendan Kellog
Damn, Mack, you shoot bastard?! I just saw it on the tv news. The police are looking for a short pudgy dude in a black leather jacket. Is that u?!

01-20-YR-3 9:26 pm

lol. Not me who pulled the trigger. I got the hell out of there though. Got maced. That stuff burns. Otherwise I'm ok. Headed home.

01-20-YR-3 9:27 pm

Emily Hodgman
We're getting our stories straight. Not to worry

01-20-YR-3 9:26 pm

Brendan Kellog
my goodness. There's a storm brewing!

01-21-YR-3 09:00 pm

Brendan Kellog
HOLY SMOKES! MACK! MACK! SAW YOUR NAME ON THE NEWS! YOU NEED TO GO DARK!

01-21-YR-3 10:05 pm

We turned ourselves in. they have my phone now, so please no more communication. We're complying with their investigation and just need to be silent publicly. Do not publicly id me please. Keep to yourself. I will contact you eventually in person.

Exhibit D

Photograph of Line to Enter Maximus Rossi's Rally

Line to Enter

Exhibit E

Photograph of Anti-Authoritarian Coalition ("Antiac") Members Entering Red Plaza

Photograph of Altercation Between Mack Hodgman and Unknown Man

Photograph of Mack Hodgman Between Ari Sinclair and Antiac Members

Photograph of Emily Hodgman Reaching Under Back of Jacket

Exhibit H

Photograph of Mack Speaking to Other Rossi Rally Attendees

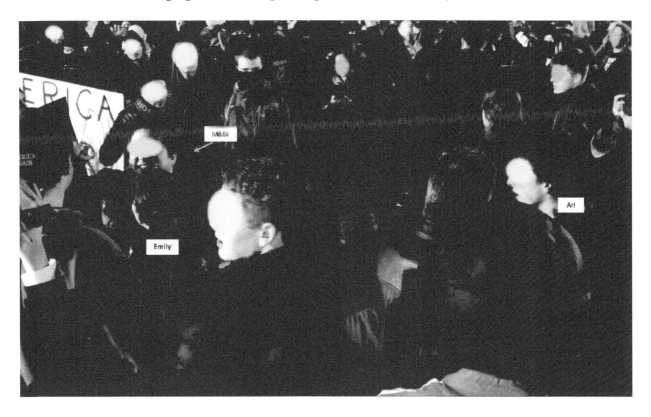

Exhibit I #1

Photograph of Rossi Rally Attendee Holding "Jorge the Toad" Flag

Exhibit I #2

Photograph of Jeremy in Crowd

Photographs of Altercation Between Jeremy and the Hodgmans

#1

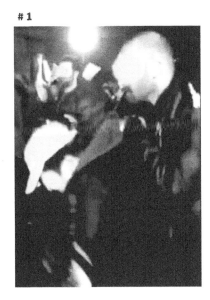

#2

#3

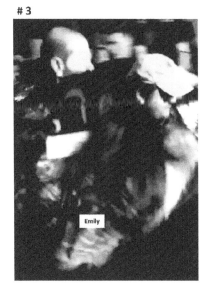

Continued Photographs of Altercation Between Jeremy and the Hodgmans

1

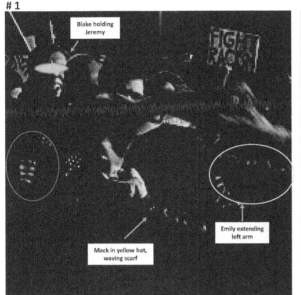

2

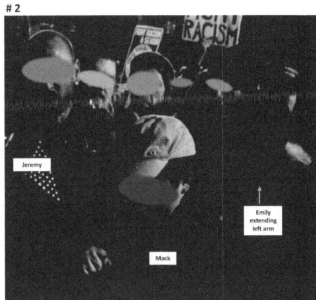

Photograph of Karambit Folding Knife with Quick-Draw Ring

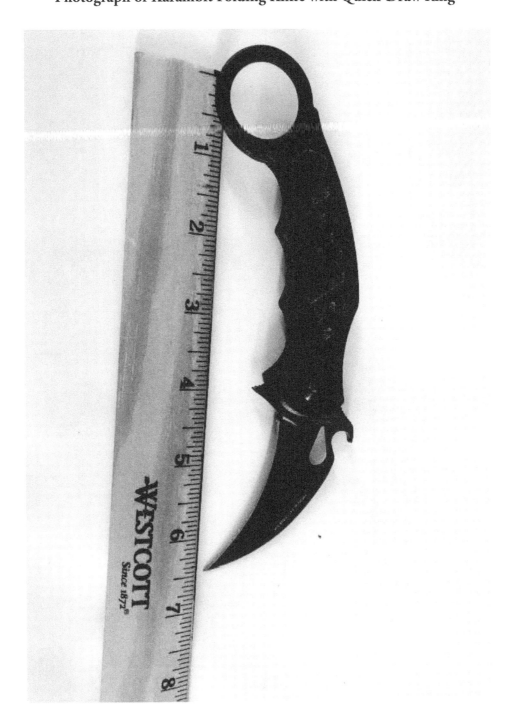

Exhibit M #1–2

Photographs of Glock Semiautomatic Pistol in Paddle Holster

1

2

Exhibit N #1–2

Photographs of Guardian Angel Pepper Spray Gun

1

#2

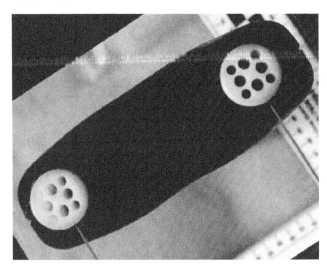

**Photograph of Mack Holding Guardian Angel Pepper Spray Gun During
Altercation with Jeremy**

Photographs of Benchmade Folding Knife from Jeremy's Pocket

1

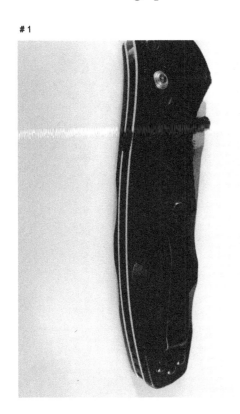

2

Photographs of Leatherman Utility Tool Taken from Waistband of Jeremy's Jeans

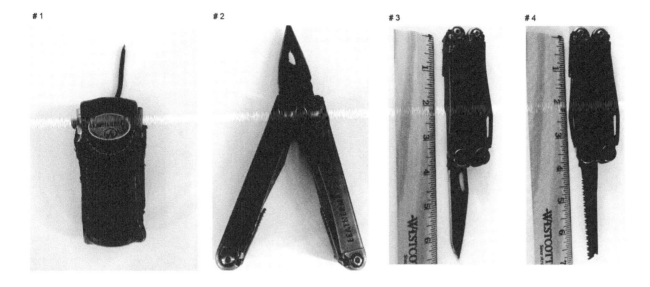

Photograph of Jeremy's Boot

Photograph of Handkerchief Found in Jeremy's Back Pocket

Diagram of Red Plaza

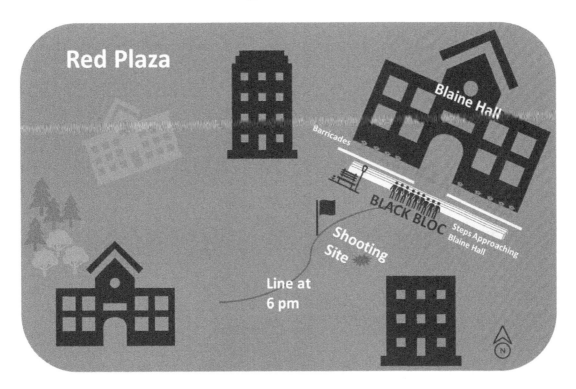

Diagram of Body's Response to Threats

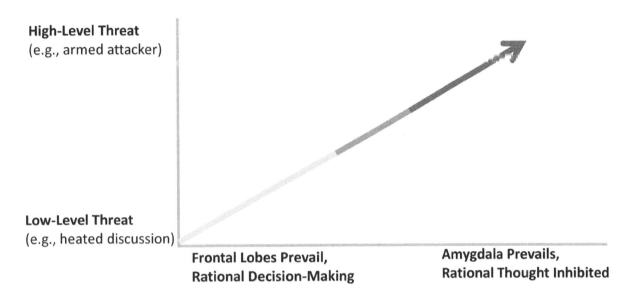

Body's Response to Threats

High-Level Threat
(e.g., armed attacker)

Low-Level Threat
(e.g., heated discussion)

**Frontal Lobes Prevail,
Rational Decision-Making**

**Amygdala Prevails,
Rational Thought Inhibited**

JURY INSTRUCTIONS

1.01   Final Instructions

Members of the jury, you are officers of this court. Base your verdict on the evidence and the law. Do not let your emotions, prejudice, or personal preference affect your decision. Accept the law from my instructions, regardless of what you personally believe the law is or should be.

1.02   Presumption of Innocence

The defendant is presumed innocent. The presumption continues throughout the course of the trial. The prosecution has the burden of proving each element of the crime charged beyond a reasonable doubt. The defendant has no burden of proving that a reasonable doubt exists. A reasonable doubt is one for which a reason exists and may arise from the evidence or lack of evidence.

1.03   The Evidence

The evidence that you are to consider consists of witness testimony, stipulations, and exhibits. As jurors, you are the sole judges of the credibility of each witness. In considering a witness's credibility, you may consider the quality of the witness's testimony, the manner of the witness while testifying, any personal interest that the witness might have in the outcome of the case, any bias or prejudice, and any other factor that affects your evaluation of the testimony.

1.04   Expert Testimony

You are not required to accept expert opinion. In considering what weight or value to give the opinion you may consider the witness's education, training, experience, knowledge, and any other factor relevant to evaluating the testimony.

1.05   Absent Witnesses

If the prosecution did not call a potential witness to testify, you may infer that person's testimony would have been unfavorable to the prosecution so long as four conditions are met: 1) the person is available to testify; 2) the testimony would have been important to the prosecution's charge; 3) it appears in the interest of the prosecution to call the witness; and 4) the witness's absence was not reasonably explained.

1.06   Hearsay Limiting Instruction

Some of the evidence admitted in this case consists of messages that the prosecution alleges were sent from Mack Hodgman's and Brendan Kellog's Facebook accounts. These statements may not be considered for the truth of the matter asserted. Any discussion of the evidence during your deliberations must be consistent with this limitation.

1.07 Elements of the Crime

In order to convict the defendant of the crime of assault in the first degree, you must be convinced that the following elements have been proved beyond a reasonable doubt:

1) **On January 20, YR-3, the defendant assaulted Jeremy Dane;**
2) **The assault was committed with a firearm;**
3) **The defendant acted with intent to inflict great bodily harm; and**
4) **This act occurred in the State of Nita.**

1.08 Definition of Assault

An assault is an intentional touching, striking, or shooting of another person, with unlawful force, that is harmful or offensive.

1.09 Definition of Intent

A person acts with intent when acting with the objective or purpose to accomplish a result that constitutes a crime.

1.10 Definition of Great Bodily Harm

Great bodily harm means physical injury that causes significant, serious, permanent disfigurement or a significant, permanent loss or impairment of the function of any bodily part or organ.

1.11 Self-Defense

It is a defense to a charge of assault in the first degree that the force used was lawful. The use of force is lawful when it aids a person who the defendant reasonably believes is about to be injured. The force may not be more than is necessary. The person may only employ such force and means as a reasonable person would under similar conditions. The prosecution bears the burden of proving beyond a reasonable doubt that the force was not lawful. If you find that the prosecution has not proved the absence of this defense, it will be your duty to return a verdict of not guilty.

1.12 Actual Danger Not Required

Actual danger is not necessary for the use of force to be lawful. A person may act on appearances in defending another, so long as they believe in good faith and on reasonable grounds that another is in actual danger of injury.

1.13 Aggressor

A person who acts in defense of another and reasonably believes the other to be the innocent party and in danger is justified in using force necessary to protect that person even if, in fact, the other person was the aggressor.

1.14 Consideration of Penalty

Do not consider the possibility of a penalty in rendering your verdict.

1.15 Concluding Instruction

Begin your deliberations by selecting a foreperson. Fill in the blank on the verdict form the words "guilty" or "not guilty" depending on your verdict. You must be unanimous in reaching your verdict. Notify the bailiff once you have reached a verdict.

IN THE DISTRICT COURT OF THE COUNTY OF DARROW

THE STATE OF NITA   )
)   Case No. YR-3–62–80
Plaintiff,   )
)
v.   )   JURY VERDICT
)
EMILY ROSE HODGMAN,   )
)
Defendant.   )

We, the jury, find the defendant EMILY ROSE HODGMAN _____ (write in
"not guilty" or "guilty") of the crime of Assault in the First Degree.

_____   _____
Date   Presiding Juror

Made in United States
North Haven, CT
04 January 2025

63988700R00065